First How Things Work
Encyclopedia

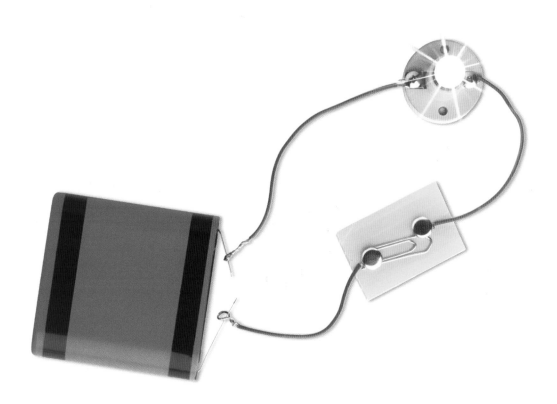

REVISED EDITION
Project editor Olivia Stanford
Editor Radhika Haswani
Senior designer Nidhi Mehra
US Senior editor Shannon Beatty
US Editor Lindsay Walter-Greaney
DTP designer Dheeraj Singh
Picture researcher Sumedha Chopra
Jacket co-ordinator Isobel Walsh
Jacket designer Kartik Gera
Managing editors Laura Gilbert, Alka Thakur Hazarika
Managing art editors Diane Peyton Jones, Romi Chakraborty
Producer Inderjit Bhullar
Pre-production producer Sophie Chatellier
Delhi team head Malavika Talukder
Creative director Helen Senior
Publishing director Sarah Larter

Consultant Jack Challoner

ORIGINAL EDITION
Senior editors Carrie Love, Penny Smith
Senior designer Rachael Grady
Design team Lauren Rosier, Pamela Shiels,
Karen Hood, Hedi Gutt, Mary Sandberg, Sadie Thomas,
Claire Patane, Laura Roberts-Jensen, and Poppy Joslin
Editorial team Lorrie Mack, Elinor Greenwood, Alexander Cox,
Fleur Star, Caroline Bingham, Wendy Horobin, and Ben Morgan
Consultant Roger Bridgman
Publishing manager Bridget Giles
Art director Rachael Foster

This American Edition, 2019
First American Edition, 2010
Published in the United States by DK Publishing
1450 Broadway, Suite 801, New York, NY 10018

Copyright © 2010, 2019 Dorling Kindersley Limited
DK, a Division of Penguin Random House LLC
19 20 21 22 23 10 9 8 7 6 5 4 3 2 1
001–280455–July/2019

A catalog record for this book
is available from the Library of Congress.
ISBN 978-1-4654-4349-6

DK books are available at special discounts when purchased in bulk
for sales promotions, premiums, fund-raising, or educational use.
For details, contact: DK Publishing Special Markets,
1450 Broadway, 8th Floor, New York, NY 10018
SpecialSales@dk.com

Printed and bound in China

A WORLD OF IDEAS:
SEE ALL THERE IS TO KNOW

www.dk.com

Contents

There is a question at the bottom of each page...

About this book

The pages of this book have special features that will show you how to get your hands on as much information as possible! Look out for these:

The Picture detective quiz will get you searching through each section for the answers.

Turn and learn buttons tell you which pages to turn to in order to find more information on each subject.

Every page is color-coded to show you which section it is in.

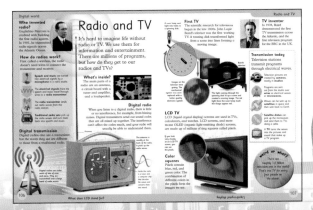

weird or what?
These buttons give extra weird and wonderful facts.

Inventions

Any new idea or product that has been created by a person can be called an invention. Inventions change the way people live their lives—they can make things safer, easier, faster, or cheaper.

Accidental ideas

Inventions can happen by accident. When chemist John Wesley Hyatt was trying to find a material for billiard balls, he spilled a liquid that dried into a tough, flexible film. This "celluloid" was later used as camera film.

Knowing your stuff

Technology is the science of how things work. The inventors of the shoes shown in this drawing knew that a coiled spring is a source of stored energy. They used this technology to make power shoes.

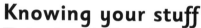

Expensive origins

Some of the things in everyday use were developed for space programs. Smoke detectors, for example, were first used on the *Skylab* space station.

"Discovery consists of seeing what everybody has seen and...

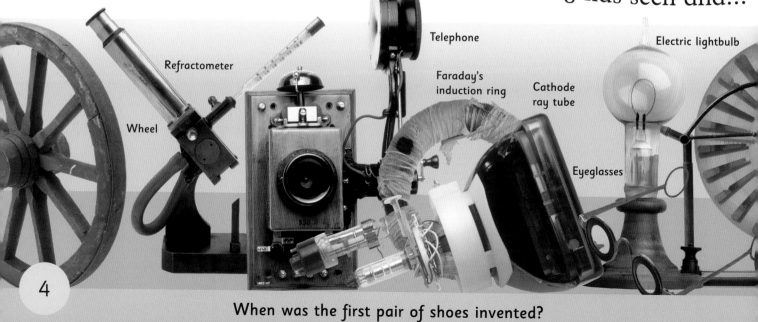

Wheel

Refractometer

Telephone

Faraday's induction ring

Cathode ray tube

Electric lightbulb

Eyeglasses

When was the first pair of shoes invented?

I can find a use for that!

Some inventions end up very different from what was planned. Scientist Dr. Spencer Silver invented a glue that wasn't sticky enough, so he thought it was useless. But his coworker Art Fry used it to stick bookmarks into his hymnal. The bookmarks wouldn't fall out, but they could be moved around. And so the sticky note was born!

Inventors

Inventors are creative people. The Italian artist and scientist Leonardo da Vinci was an avid inventor. He designed hundreds of machines, including airplanes, pumps, and cannons, that were centuries ahead of their time.

Leonardo da Vinci sketched a design for a helicopter 500 years before the first successful plane flight.

The first military helicopter, designed by Igor Sikorsky, took to the skies in the 1940s.

How long does an invention take?

An invention has to begin with an idea. It can sometimes take hundreds of years before the science, technology, or materials are advanced enough to make the idea work. The idea for a helicopter may have come from China as far back as 400 BCE.

... thinking what nobody else has thought." —Albert Szent-Györgyi

Wimhurst voltage generator

Tea maker

Microscope

Camera

Electric guitar

People in Mesopotamia made the first leather shoes in 1500 BCE.

Better by design

Anyone can be an inventor. Many successful inventions came from engineers who used their knowledge of materials (such as iron) to try new things.

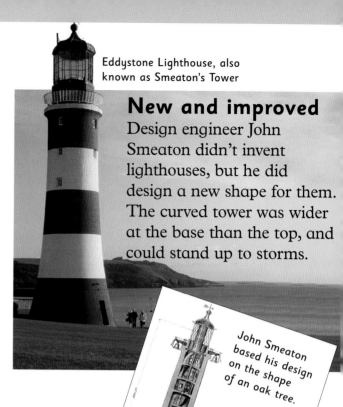

Eddystone Lighthouse, also known as Smeaton's Tower

New and improved

Design engineer John Smeaton didn't invent lighthouses, but he did design a new shape for them. The curved tower was wider at the base than the top, and could stand up to storms.

John Smeaton based his design on the shape of an oak tree.

US inventor Thomas Edison patented an amazing 1,093 inventions.

That was my idea!

If someone thinks their idea is good, they can patent it. Patents are official documents that describe the idea and show who came up with it, so no one else can steal it and say it's theirs.

From that...

Since the telephone was invented in 1876, people have changed its design to make it better. Early telephones were large and boxy. Making a call may have involved winding a handle or turning a dial.

Who is often called the "father of the cell phone"?

Meet an engineer

Isambard Kingdom Brunel was a 19th-century British engineer who designed bridges, tunnels, ships, and even an entire railroad. He worked a lot with iron and knew it could be used in ways that had never been tried before.

Brunel's Royal Albert Railway Bridge was built in 1859. It's the only one of its kind.

Will it sell?

Inventions can succeed or fail depending on whether or not people want them.

Sneakers were a success! Can you imagine playing a sport in any other shoes?

LEGO® was a success! These plastic bricks are one of the best-selling toys in the world.

Microwave ovens were a success! They completely changed the way many people cook.

Sinclair C5 was a failure. Not many people wanted to buy a battery-powered tricycle.

Making a difference

The way something looks can be just as important as how it works. The first Apple iMac's colorful design made it stand out among other computers, so more people bought it.

... to this!

Today's cell phones are small by comparison, and they can do much more than just make phone calls. You don't even need to use your hands to call a friend on some of them.

What will they think of next?

The American engineer and inventor Martin Cooper.

Early inventions

Some discoveries and inventions seem so basic it's hard to imagine life without them. Yet, someone had to be the first to create fire, wheels, shoes, and paper.

c. 7000 BCE
For the first time, people knew how to start a **fire**. Later, they would learn to use fire in metalwork to create tools.

c. 3500 BCE
The first **wheel** was made from solid wood. Experts think it was invented in Mesopotamia (modern-day Iraq).

c. 2500 BCE
Early welding involved hammering heated metal parts together until they fused. As a result, all kinds of metal objects could be made.

c. 2000 BCE
Spoked wheels were lighter and more useful than solid ones. Two-wheeled chariots could move very fast.

7000 BCE

2250 BCE

c. 3000 BCE
Reed pens and brushes were used by the ancient Egyptians for drawing symbols on papyrus (which was used before the invention of paper).

c. 1700 BCE
Evidence of early **plumbing** (drains and pipes) can be found among the ruins of the Palace of Knossos, on the island of Crete.

c. 6500 BCE
Before mirrors were made, people would see their reflections in pools of still water. The first **mirrors** were created from highly polished obsidian, a type of volcanic stone.

c. 6000 BCE
The ancient Egyptians used bundles of papyrus reeds to make **reed boats**. They used the boats for trade.

c. 4000 BCE
Wooden **plows** were pulled by animals to cut and turn soil for farming.

What does the "c." in "c. 6000" mean?

c. 1000 BCE
The earliest **underfloor heating system** was found in modern-day Alaska. The Romans invented their own system in Europe about 500 years later.

c. 500 BCE
The Greek **abacus** was a table with counters that people used to make calculations. Today's familiar abacus with rods and beads was invented in China almost 2,000 years later.

c. 300 BCE
The Chinese discovered that a free-moving magnet will point north—and so the compass was born.

c. 1000 BCE
The first **magnets** were simply lumps of magnetite, a naturally occurring magnetic mineral. Most modern magnets are synthetic.

c. 50 BCE
Paper was invented in China more than 2,000 years ago, but the invention was kept a secret for 700 years.

1200 BCE

100 BCE

c. 1500 BCE
Most early peoples wore sandals, but in Mesopotamia people crafted leather **shoes** to protect their feet.

c. 640 BCE
The earliest **coins** were used in ancient Greece, India, and China. Before this, goods would be exchanged for other items.

c. 200 BCE
The **Archimedes screw** is named after the Greek scientist Archimedes, who explained that water can travel upward along a turning screw.

c. 20 BCE
Although glass-making had been around for more than 2,000 years, the invention of **glass-blowing** in Syria made it possible to create glass items in many shapes.

c. 1200 BCE
The first **ships** were built by Phoenicians and Greeks to carry large amounts of cargo for trade.

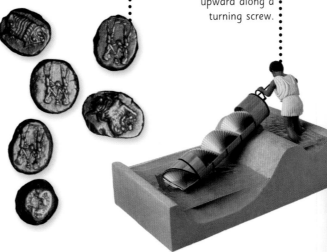

9

It stands for "circa," which means "approximately."

Modern technology

Today, the phrase "modern technology" is usually used to mean computers. But a few hundred years ago, steam power and mechanical presses were new and exciting technology.

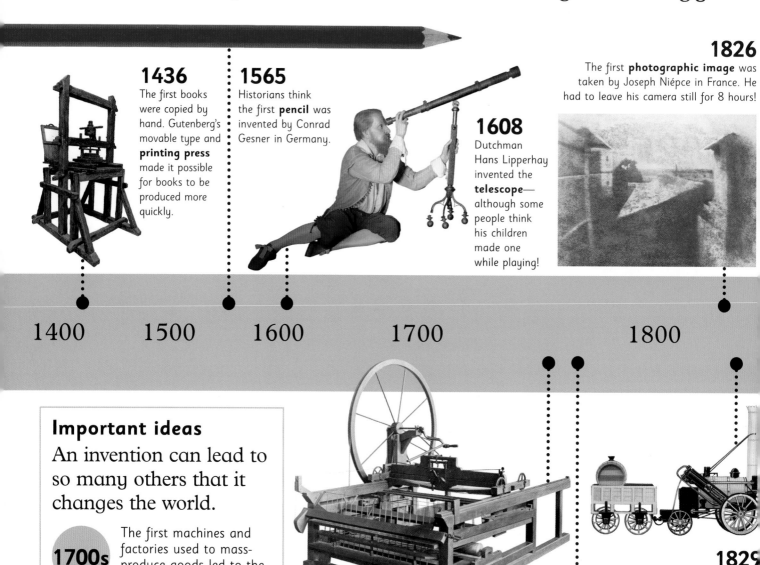

1436
The first books were copied by hand. Gutenberg's movable type and **printing press** made it possible for books to be produced more quickly.

1565
Historians think the first **pencil** was invented by Conrad Gesner in Germany.

1608
Dutchman Hans Lipperhay invented the **telescope**— although some people think his children made one while playing!

1826
The first **photographic image** was taken by Joseph Niépce in France. He had to leave his camera still for 8 hours!

1400	1500	1600	1700	1800

Important ideas

An invention can lead to so many others that it changes the world.

1700s
The first machines and factories used to mass-produce goods led to the **Industrial Revolution**.

1800s
For the first time, people could safely harness the power of **electricity**.

1970s
The **microprocessor** made computers smaller and started the Information Age.

1764
James Hargreaves' **spinning jenny** made thread for cloth faster than ever before.

1769
James Watt's improved **steam engine** was used to power all kinds of machines.

1829
Stephenson's Rocke[t] pulled the first successfu[l] **steam train**. It reache[d] a top speed of abou[t] 28 mph (45 kph).

Why was the printing press so important?

1903
The **first powered flight** took place in the US. The plane, the *Wright Flyer*, was made of wood and cloth.

1977
The first **personal computers** were large, chunky machines that had very little memory compared to today's models.

1878
The **lightbulb** was invented around the same time in two different countries—by Thomas Edison in the US and Joseph Swan in Britain.

1957
The Soviet Union's *Sputnik 1* was the first man-made **space satellite**.

1876
Alexander Graham Bell got the first patent for a **telephone**, although others nearly beat him to it.

1926
The **televisor** was the first kind of television. It was replaced by electronic television in the 1930s.

2012
3-D printers have made it possible to manufacture solid objects from digital information.

1900

2000

1885
Karl Benz made the first **gas-powered car** in Germany. By 1896, there were 130 Benz cars on the roads.

WWW

1990
The invention of the **World Wide Web** meant that anyone could get information from across the world over the Internet.

1895
German scientist Wilhelm Röntgen (accidentally) discovered the **X-ray**.

1998
The first handheld **e-book reader** could store 10 books or 4,000 pages.

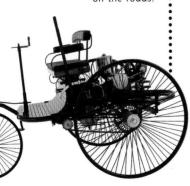

1979
This year saw the first public **cell-phone system**, in Japan.

1938
Laszlo and Georg Biró's **ballpoint pen** had fast-drying ink and didn't need to be refilled very often.

2010
The **iPad**®, a type of touchscreen, mobile computer with a built-in battery, is one of the most popular tablets.

iPad® mini

11

Technology all around us

The use of science to create new and better machines and ways of doing things is called technology. Every day you use technology in one of its many different forms. Here are a few of them.

Which technology is your favorite?

Turn and learn
Space travel:
pp. 54–55
Robots:
pp. 114–115

Mechanical
Mechanical technology is the design, production, and use of machines, such as wind-up clocks and other appliances that do not use electrical, electronic, or computer technology.

Chemical technology is used to make plastics and refine crude oil.

Chemical
Using the science of chemistry to turn raw materials into more useful things, such as plastics, cosmetics, or medicine, is called chemical technology.

Electrical
Technology that deals with electrical circuits and equipment is known as electrical technology. It is commonly used in the design and construction of electronic gadgets, such as cell phones and televisions, and power grids.

How does nanotechnology get its name?

Digital

In digital technology, information is recorded using combinations of 0 and 1 to represent words and pictures. This system allows huge amounts of data to be squeezed into tiny spaces.

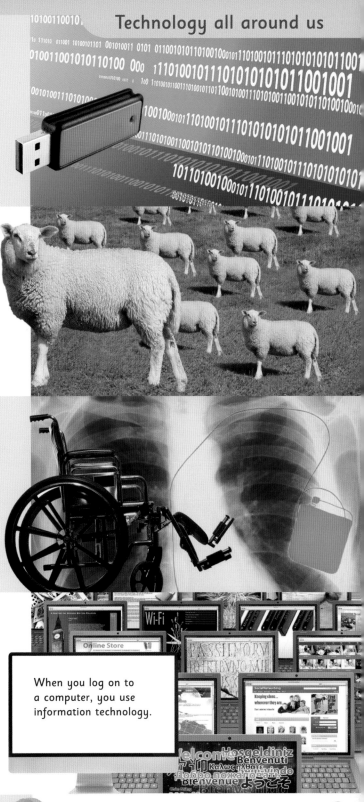

Biotechnology

This term refers to technology that is based on biology—the study of living things. Biotechnology is commonly used in agriculture and food production. Genetic engineering is one kind of biotechnology.

Medical

Anything (such as a tool, machine, process, or substance) that is used to diagnose, observe, treat, cure, or prevent people's illnesses or injuries comes under the heading of medical technology.

Information

The study, design, and use of electronic information systems is known as information technology. The term covers machines such as computers (hardware) and the programs they run (software).

When you log on to a computer, you use information technology.

Nanotechnology

Modern science can create materials and simple machines much too small for you to see under a normal microscope. This nanotechnology is used in products such as special sunscreens and textiles.

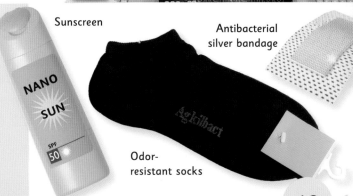

Sunscreen

Antibacterial silver bandage

Odor-resistant socks

13

From the Greek word "nano," which originally meant "dwarf."

Simple machines

It's hard to hit a nail into wood with your hand, but much easier with a hammer. Tools, such as this one, are called simple machines. They help people work faster and better.

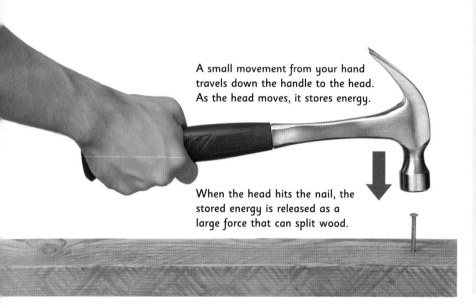

A small movement from your hand travels down the handle to the head. As the head moves, it stores energy.

When the head hits the nail, the stored energy is released as a large force that can split wood.

Feel the force

Tools, levers, and pulleys are all simple machines. They increase the size of the force you apply, so you can perform a job with less effort. When you use a hammer, you need to move the handle only a small amount to give the head enough energy to push the nail through wood.

Levers move loads

Levers are simple machines with a solid part that turns around a fixed point, called the fulcrum. They help magnify or reduce a force. There are three different types of lever: class 1, class 2, and class 3.

Class 1 lever

In class 1 levers, the fulcrum is in the middle. The force you apply at one end can be magnified at the other end.

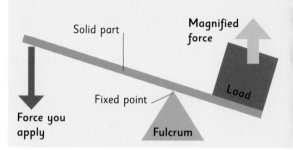

Solid part

Magnified force

Force you apply

Fixed point

Load

Fulcrum

Class 2 lever

In class 2 levers, the fulcrum is at one end and your hands apply a force at the other end. This creates a magnified force in the middle.

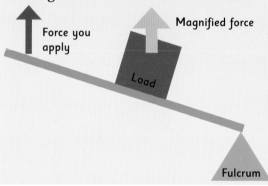

Force you apply

Magnified force

Load

Fulcrum

Class 3 lever

A class 3 lever reduces the force applied between the load and fulcrum. They are used in tweezers and other tools that pick up small, delicate objects.

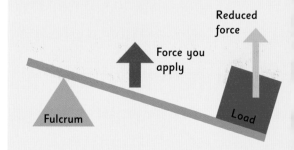

Reduced force

Force you apply

Fulcrum

Load

14

air of scissors is made of two class 1
rs. You apply force with your fingers,
this force is magnified at the blades,
ng them the power they need to cut
ough paper or other materials.

Fulcrum

wheelbarrow is a class 2 lever. It
agnifies the weak force from your
rms to pick up the heavy load.

Fulcrum

Fulcrum

he fulcrum in this pair of chopsticks
at the point where the girl holds
em. Her fingers apply the force
at opens and closes the chopsticks
pick up food.

Pulley power

Pulleys are used to lift heavy
loads. A pulley is a length of rope
wrapped around one or more
wheels. Adding wheels to the
pulley system creates more lifting
force—but you have to pull the
rope farther to lift the load.

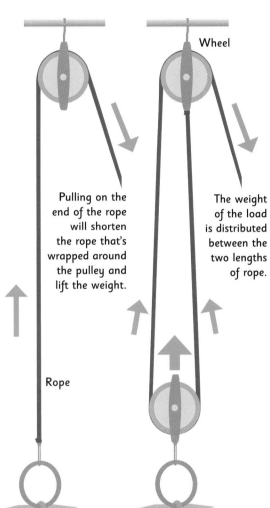

Wheel

Pulling on the
end of the rope
will shorten
the rope that's
wrapped around
the pulley and
lift the weight.

The weight
of the load
is distributed
between the
two lengths
of rope.

Rope

Load

Load

**Pulley with
single wheel**

**Pulley with
multiple wheels**

Turn and learn
Cranes:
pp. 18–19
Conveyors:
pp. 20–21

Picture detective

Look through the Hard
at work pages and see
if you can identify the
picture clues below.

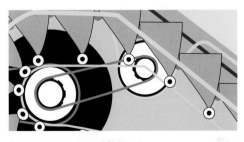

The power that makes things move or stop. Simply, a push or a pull.

Using levers

Every time you open a door, ride a bike, or even bend your arm, you are using levers. Many of the objects we use every day depend on leverage to magnify forces and make tasks easier.

Magnifying forces

The amount by which a lever magnifies a force depends on how far the force you apply and the force the lever produces are from the fulcrum.

Levers at home

These are all compound levers—tools made up of more than one lever.

Nutcrackers are a pair of class 2 levers that are joined at the fulcrum.

Tweezers are made up of two class 3 levers. They reduce the force you apply.

Pliers comprise of two class 1 levers. They magnify the force applied on the handles.

If the force you apply is the same distance from the fulcrum as the force the lever produces, the two forces are equal.

If the force you apply is twice as far from the fulcrum as the force the lever produces, the lever doubles the force.

If the force you apply is three times as far from the fulcrum as the force the lever produces, the lever triples the force.

Crowbar

One of the simplest kinds of lever is the crowbar, which is a class 1 lever. You use a crowbar to pry very heavy objects off the ground. The longer the crowbar is, the more the force is magnified at the other end. However, you have to move the long end of the crowbar much farther than the short end will move.

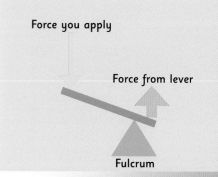

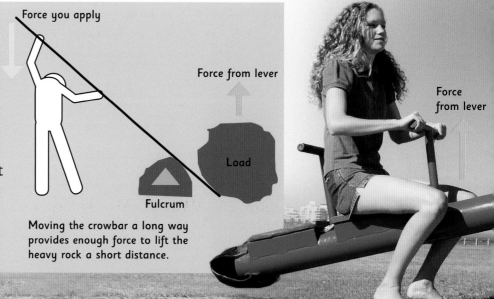

Moving the crowbar a long way provides enough force to lift the heavy rock a short distance.

What class of lever do bottle openers and tongs fall under?

Human body

Your arms and legs can act as levers. When you stand on tiptoes, your lower leg works like a class 2 lever. The powerful calf muscle pulls up your heel, lifting your body weight (the load), while your toes form the fulcrum.

Force you apply

Load

Fulcrum

Fishing rod

When you use a fishing rod to cast a line, the rod works like a class 3 lever. Your hand applies a powerful force near the base of the rod to create a smaller force at the tip of the rod. Although the force is weaker, the tip moves much farther and faster than your hands, magnifying the speed.

Force you apply

Fulcrum

Load

The rod also works as a class 3 lever when you haul in a fish.

Seesaw

A seesaw is a class 1 lever. You use the force of your body weight to move the seesaw. If two people of equal weight sit at equal distance from the fulcrum, their weight will balance. But if one of them sits farther from the fulcrum, their weight is magnified and the seesaw tips over.

A small child could balance the weight of an elephant by sitting far enough away from the fulcrum.

Force you apply

Fulcrum

17

Bottle openers are class 2 levers. Tongs are class 3 compound levers.

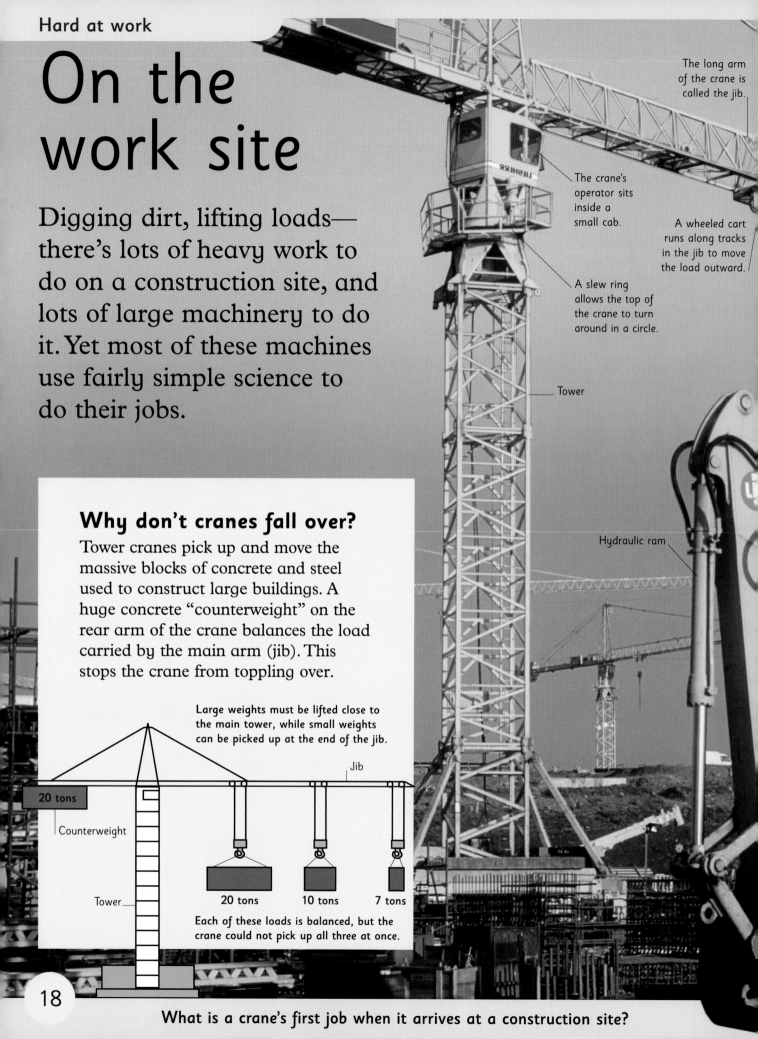

On the work site

Digging dirt, lifting loads—there's lots of heavy work to do on a construction site, and lots of large machinery to do it. Yet most of these machines use fairly simple science to do their jobs.

The long arm of the crane is called the jib.

The crane's operator sits inside a small cab.

A wheeled cart runs along tracks in the jib to move the load outward.

A slew ring allows the top of the crane to turn around in a circle.

Tower

Hydraulic ram

Why don't cranes fall over?

Tower cranes pick up and move the massive blocks of concrete and steel used to construct large buildings. A huge concrete "counterweight" on the rear arm of the crane balances the load carried by the main arm (jib). This stops the crane from toppling over.

Large weights must be lifted close to the main tower, while small weights can be picked up at the end of the jib.

Jib

20 tons

Counterweight

Tower

20 tons   10 tons   7 tons

Each of these loads is balanced, but the crane could not pick up all three at once.

What is a crane's first job when it arrives at a construction site?

Pulleys in action

Cranes lift objects with a hook and pulley. A steel cable is looped around pulley wheels on the hook and jib, and wound in by a motor in the crane's rear arm. Each loop of cable magnifies the crane's lifting force.

Diggers

Diggers use a set of connected levers to scoop earth out of the ground. The levers are joined like the parts of a human arm, the bucket forming the "hand." They are moved by hydraulic rams—metal tubes that extend as oil is pumped into them.

Hydraulic cranes

Mobile cranes, such as those on fire engines, are hydraulic cranes. Like diggers, they use hydraulic rams to apply the force needed to lift loads. By varying the size of the metal tubes in the rams, the hydraulic system can produce huge lifting forces—enough to raise bridges, trains, and even entire buildings.

Like pulleys and levers, hydraulic rams can magnify forces.

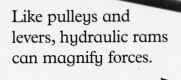

When the bucket is pushed inward, its sharp teeth dig into the ground to scoop out dirt.

Boom

Slew ring

The slew ring at the base of the arm allows the arm to rotate (turn around).

Bucket

It builds itself, adding one section at a time to its tower.

Moving stuff

From airports and factories to stores and offices, conveyors are used in all kinds of places to make it easier to move loads from one point to another.

A gravity conveyor seen from above

Move along
The simplest type of conveyor is a gravity conveyor. It is made up of lots of rollers or wheels in a frame. As each roller or wheel turns, the load gets shifted to the next.

Luggage and other cargo are moved on conveyors behind the scenes at an airport.

Up, down, and sideways
Belt conveyors can move loads up, down, and sideways. The load sits on a belt that turns around rollers, called pulleys. The drive pulley is connected to a motor, which makes it rotate.

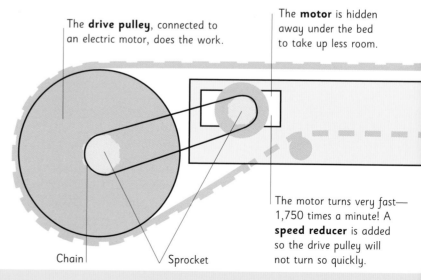

The **drive pulley**, connected to an electric motor, does the work.

The **motor** is hidden away under the bed to take up less room.

The motor turns very fast—1,750 times a minute! A **speed reducer** is added so the drive pulley will not turn so quickly.

Chain

Sprocket

When was the first escalator used?

Going up!

It's not just boxes that are moved around on conveyors— people are too. Escalators are moving staircases, with each separate step connected to a conveyor belt.

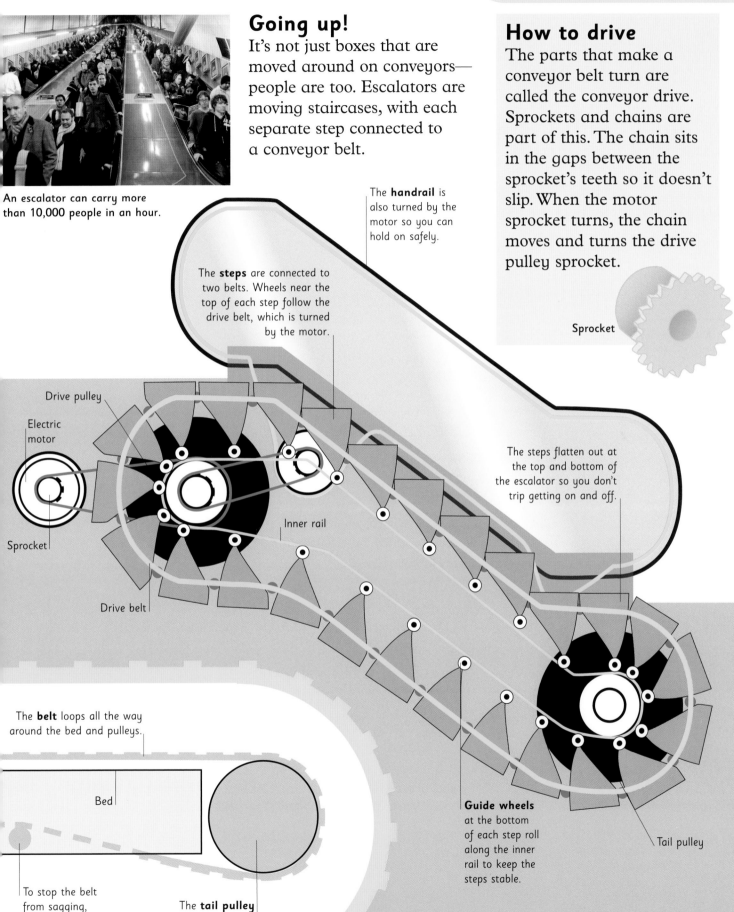

An escalator can carry more than 10,000 people in an hour.

How to drive

The parts that make a conveyor belt turn are called the conveyor drive. Sprockets and chains are part of this. The chain sits in the gaps between the sprocket's teeth so it doesn't slip. When the motor sprocket turns, the chain moves and turns the drive pulley sprocket.

Sprocket

The **handrail** is also turned by the motor so you can hold on safely.

The **steps** are connected to two belts. Wheels near the top of each step follow the drive belt, which is turned by the motor.

The steps flatten out at the top and bottom of the escalator so you don't trip getting on and off.

Drive pulley

Electric motor

Sprocket

Inner rail

Drive belt

The **belt** loops all the way around the bed and pulleys.

Bed

To stop the belt from sagging, it is sometimes tucked around small rollers called **return idlers**.

The **tail pulley** is turned by the moving belt.

Guide wheels at the bottom of each step roll along the inner rail to keep the steps stable.

Tail pulley

21

The first working model was made in the US in 1895 and used as a fairground ride!

Getting around = Energy

We can all use our legs for getting around, but they're a bit slow and won't take us far without making us tired. What we need is something that can get us from one place to another fast—a vehicle of some sort.

But what does it take to get a car racing along a road?

Turn and learn

How bicycles work: **pp. 26–27**
Car engines: **pp. 32–33**

Energy sources
To move or do any kind of work you need energy. We get energy from our food; vehicles use fuel or electricity.

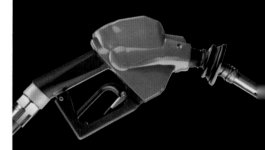

Energy-rich oil
One of the best sources of energy is oil. When oil is burned, it releases lots of energy.

Types of fuel
Vehicles can get their energy from many different types of fuel.

 Gas is made from crude oil. Most cars run on gas burned in the engine.

 Diesel is also made from crude oil. It produces more energy than gas.

 Electricity can be used to power some cars but is mainly used by trains.

 Solar energy comes from the sun. It can be stored for use by cars.

What moves faster than anything else in the universe?

Force ▶ Movement

Getting going
Once you have enough energy, you can use it to create forces that will help you move. Forces are simply pushes or pulls.

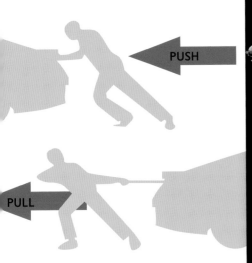

PUSH

PULL

Wheels turn by using opposing forces. As the tire pushes back against the road, the road pushes the wheel forward.

Friction
Friction is a force that stops things from moving by pulling them in the other direction. Without its gripping action, you wouldn't be able to walk or drive anywhere.

On the move
With its engine turned off, friction will slow a vehicle to a stop. To keep it moving, the engine must keep turning the wheels.

Speeding up
Increasing the speed at which an engine turns the wheels will make the vehicle go faster. This is usually done by increasing the flow of fuel to the engine.

Brakes work by pushing pads or discs against the wheels.

Slowing down
Brakes have pads made of high-friction materials; pressing the pads against the wheels slows the vehicle down to a stop.

Picture detective
Look through the Getting around pages and see if you can identify the picture clues below.

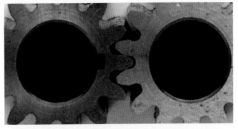

23

Wheels and axles

An axle is a simple rod that connects two wheels. For nearly 6,000 years, the wheel and axle have made it easy to move objects.

Friction

Friction is the force created when two surfaces touch. As you slide an object, you create a lot of friction. When you roll it on wheels, you create less.

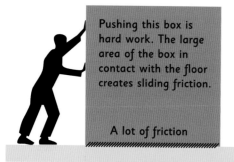

Pushing this box is hard work. The large area of the box in contact with the floor creates sliding friction.

A lot of friction

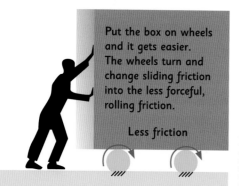

Put the box on wheels and it gets easier. The wheels turn and change sliding friction into the less forceful, rolling friction.

Less friction

Fixed axle

A fixed axle can be found on simple carts. The axle is attached to the cart and the wheels turn independently, allowing the cart to move.

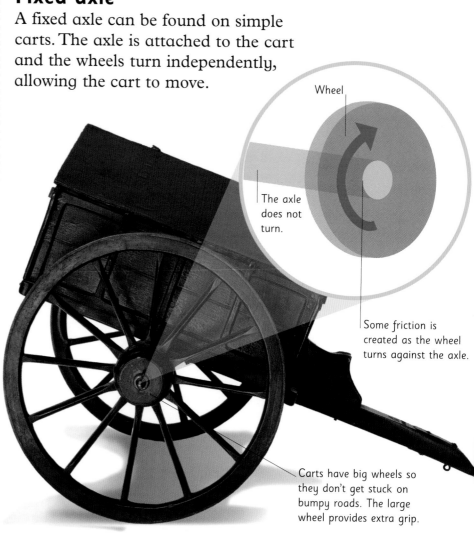

Wheel

The axle does not turn.

Some friction is created as the wheel turns against the axle.

Carts have big wheels so they don't get stuck on bumpy roads. The large wheel provides extra grip.

Wheels of history

Historians believe the very first wheels were used 7,000 years ago by potters to make pots. Later, the wheel was used to help move and transport objects.

The first use of wheels and an axle was on horse-drawn chariots around 3500 BCE.

Bicycles, which allow us to create our own power, have been popular for nearly 200 years.

What is the largest wheel in the world?

Spoke support

The little rods that connect the outer rim to the inner hub of the wheel are called spokes. They make the wheel lighter, yet strong enough to take the weight. They also spread the weight evenly and transfer power from the axle.

Outer rim · Spoke · Hub

Other wheels

Wheels don't just move you or your belongings. They have a diverse range of uses.

 A steering wheel is the fifth wheel on a car and helps guide it.

 Gears use interlocking "teeth" to transfer movement and power.

 Pulleys and levers use wheels to help move heavy objects.

 Waterwheels create mechanical energy when a river's current turns them.

Rolling axle

Modern cars and vehicles use a rolling axle system. The axle is connected to the engine and helps turn the wheels.

The wheels turn with the axle.

Gears

Axle

Driveshaft

The turning force created by the axle moves the wheel.

The engine turns a rod known as the driveshaft. This uses gears to transfer the engine's power into the axle.

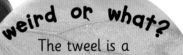

weird or what?

The tweel is a brand-new car wheel that doesn't need a tire. Instead, it uses flexible spokes, which bend with the bumps on the road. The tweel will never get a flat like a tire.

In "two-wheel drive" cars, one axle powers just two wheels. "Four-wheel drive" cars are powered by both axles, moving all four wheels.

With the invention of the engine, bigger vehicles needed bigger wheels to help move heavy cargo.

After a few early designs, the motor car was built and its wheels were covered with air-filled, rubber tires.

The modern-day wheel is a high-tech device. Racing cars use special wheels for different racing conditions.

The High Roller, a Ferris wheel in Las Vegas, stands 550 ft (167.6 m) tall.

The history of bikes

The dandy horse (1817) was the first type of bike and had no pedals at all. Riders had to push forward with their feet until they came to a downhill slope.

The velocipede (1863) had pedals that were fixed to its wheels and had no gears. This meant the wheel turned once for every turn of the pedal. It took huge effort to travel fast.

High Wheelers (1872) got around the problem of fixed pedals by having a huge front wheel. They were faster but also dangerous—it was a long fall down from the saddle.

The safety bicycle (around 1884) was the original name for a bicycle with gears. It had the same basic design as those used today.

Pedal power

A bicycle is a lean, mean travel machine. Bikes are so efficient they can turn 90 percent of the energy you put into pedaling into forward motion.

Get in gear
Bike gears are cogs (wheels with teeth) that are linked by a chain. Using different gears makes pedaling easier or faster. Bikes can have up to 30 gears.

When a small gear at the front wheel is connected to a large gear at the back, the bike is in low gear. This turns the wheel slowly but forcefully, so is ideal for traveling uphill.

When a large gear at the front wheel is connected to a small gear at the back, the bike is in high gear. The wheel will turn several times for each rotation of the pedals. This is ideal for speeding along on flat land or racing downhill.

The main picture shows a BMX bike. What does BMX stand for?

Handlebars are used to control the front wheel. Moving the handlebars lets you change direction and also helps you keep your balance as you cycle along. Handlebars are levers, and the longer they are, the easier they are to turn.

Brakes work when you squeeze the brake lever on the handlebars. It pulls a cable that's connected to brake shoes on either side of the front wheel. The rubber shoes grip onto the wheel like a clamp. This creates friction against the wheel, slowing it down.

Frames of most modern bikes are the "diamond" kind—a shape made up of two triangles of hollow steel, which is light but strong.

Pedals turn the up-and-down motion of your legs into the circular movement of the wheels.

Tires have patterns called treads that increase friction between the bike wheel and the road surface, so the bike is easy to control and keeps a good grip, even in rainy conditions.

Wheels have spokes that carry the weight of the bike and the rider.

weird or what?

The world's longest true bicycle (one with just two wheels) was built in the Netherlands in 2002. It was 92 ft (28 m) long!

Bike types

Utility bikes are used for everyday cycling. A chain guard stops the oily chain from getting your clothes dirty, and bags can sit safely in the basket.

Mountain bikes have a strong frame and wide tires for extra grip on rough ground.

Track-racing bikes are designed for speed. The rider must bend low to hold the handlebars, making a streamlined shape. They have no brakes!

Recumbent bikes have frames that make the rider lean back in their seat. Some have covers, too. They can be tricky to ride, but can go very fast.

27

Bicycle Motocross, a cycling sport in which BMX bicycles are used for racing and stunt riding.

Holding the road

Why do trucks and tractors need such big wheels? It's to help them get a grip on slippery surfaces and move easily while pulling loads.

Sticking to the surface

Heavy vehicles need big tires to help spread the weight of the trucks and their loads. The tires move the vehicle using friction. As the tires press down and backward on the road, the road pushes the vehicle forward.

Losing your grip

This car's wheels can't get enough grip to move on a muddy road. Mud is wet, slimy, and does not have any snags or bumps to provide friction. Also, the car's small and smooth wheels do not provide enough surface area to reduce the pressure of the car's heavy weight on the ground. You're stuck!

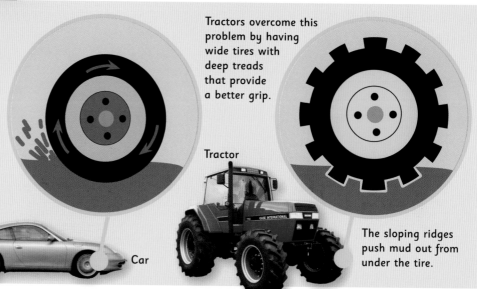

Tractors overcome this problem by having wide tires with deep treads that provide a better grip.

Car

Tractor

The sloping ridges push mud out from under the tire.

28

Monster trucks

What do you get if you put the body of a pickup truck on a bus axle? A monster truck! Add some tractor wheels and a good suspension system, and you can bounce over anything.

Smoothing out the bumps

When you hit a bump in the road, your wheels move up and down. This is because of the vehicle's suspension system. It is designed to absorb the impact through the tires, springs, and shock absorbers.

Inside the shock absorber is a piston that pushes against a gas. The gas slows the piston down and turns its energy into heat.

Tire

Spring

Cross section

Shock absorber

Tires
Tires are left slightly soft so they can squash over small bumps without moving up and down.

Springs
There is a spring around each shock absorber that reduces the impact by squeezing and stretching.

Shock absorbers
These are pumps filled with gas that absorb the energy of the wheel hitting the ground.

29

It is 80 ft (24 m) tall and weighs 12 tons (11 metric tons).

Crank it up

Many forms of transportation use wheels, which push against the ground and use friction to move. But what makes the wheels turn?

Up and down, around and around

To ride a bike, you move your legs up and down on the pedals. The pedals turn cranks around and around, which turn the wheels. A car's wheels move in a similar way.

Gear

Crank

Pedal

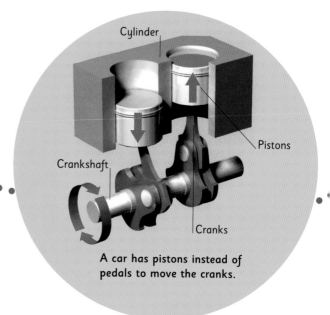

Cylinder

Pistons

Crankshaft

Cranks

A car has pistons instead of pedals to move the cranks.

Rear-wheel drive

A bike's cranks turn a chain that is connected to the back wheel, so when you pedal, you are actually powering only one wheel. Many bikes have gears to make pedaling easier.

Types of engine

Different vehicles have different numbers of cylinders. Generally, the larger the vehicle, the more they have.

A lawnmower has only one cylinder. This means only one piston goes up and down to turn the wheels.

This motorcycle has two large cylinders. Their slow up-and-down motion gives the Harley its distinctive thumping sound.

Lawnmower

Harley Davidson

How many parts are there in an average car?

Secret cylinders

There is a row of metal cylinders hidden deep in a car's engine. The pistons inside them pump up and down, just like your feet on a bike. Start at stage 1 in the diagram to see how the pistons power a car's wheels.

This car, like the bike, is driven forward by its back wheels.

4 The driveshaft turns the wheel axles and the wheel axles turn the wheels.

Axle

Axle

2 Car pistons are also attached to levers called cranks. These turn the crankshaft.

Piston

Driveshaft

3 The crankshaft turns the driveshaft through the gearbox.

1 The pistons pump up and down like legs.

Gearbox

Crankshaft

Rotation relay

The pistons are connected to the crankshaft, which, in turn, is connected to the driveshaft. The driveshaft is connected to the axles, and the wheels go around and around.

Turn and learn

Internal combustion engine: **pp. 32–33** Race cars: **pp. 34–35**

A Formula 1 racing car needs an extremely fast and powerful engine. It has 8 cylinders.

Formula 1 car

This huge cargo ship is five stories tall. It weighs over 2,500 tons (2,300 metric tons) and has 14 cylinders, each one bigger than a person.

Emma Maersk

MAERSK LINE

Around 30,000.

Engines of fire

Most cars and other vehicles burn fuel to release the energy needed to move. This happens inside an internal combustion engine—an engine that is powered by lots of little fires.

What makes it burn?

Fuels such as gasoline and diesel burn easily. All they need are a spark and oxygen, which is a gas found in the air.

Recipe for fire:

$$Fuel + Oxygen + A\ spark = Fire$$

Exploding with power

At normal speed, a car's engine lights around 50 little fires every second. The fires make pistons shoot up and down, with four "strokes" for every fire—suck, squeeze, bang, and blow.

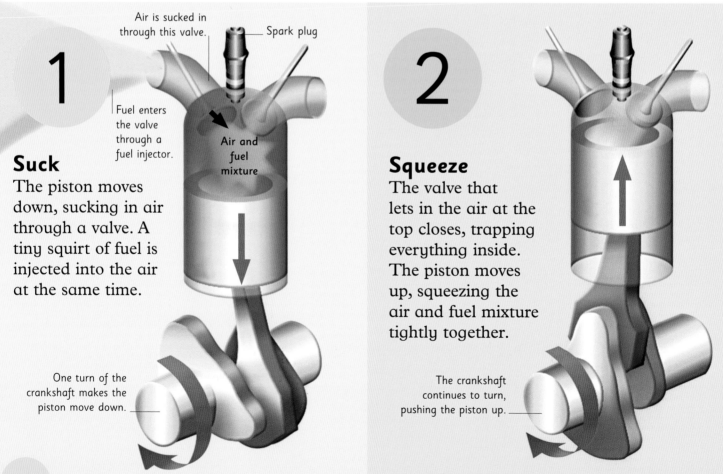

1

Air is sucked in through this valve.

Spark plug

Fuel enters the valve through a fuel injector.

Air and fuel mixture

Suck

The piston moves down, sucking in air through a valve. A tiny squirt of fuel is injected into the air at the same time.

One turn of the crankshaft makes the piston move down.

2

Squeeze

The valve that lets in the air at the top closes, trapping everything inside. The piston moves up, squeezing the air and fuel mixture tightly together.

The crankshaft continues to turn, pushing the piston up.

What actually is fire?

The cylinders

The combustion (burning) happens in an engine's cylinders. The energy released by each tiny explosion is directed to the pistons, causing them to move up and down. This drives the crankshaft around and around, which turns the wheels (see pp. 30–31).

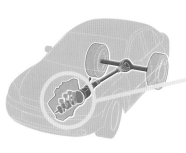

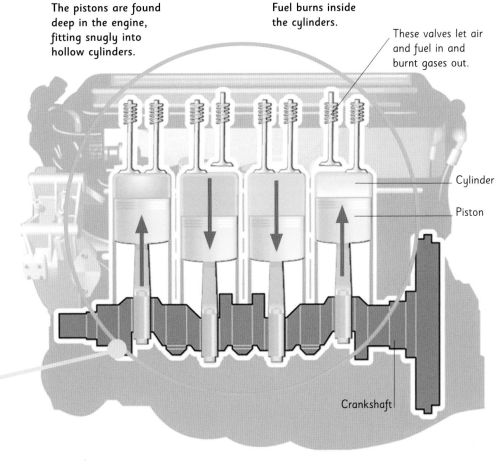

The pistons are found deep in the engine, fitting snugly into hollow cylinders.

Fuel burns inside the cylinders.

These valves let air and fuel in and burnt gases out.

Cylinder

Piston

Crankshaft

3

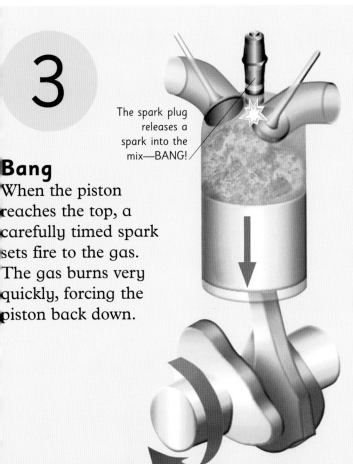

The spark plug releases a spark into the mix—BANG!

Bang

When the piston reaches the top, a carefully timed spark sets fire to the gas. The gas burns very quickly, forcing the piston back down.

4

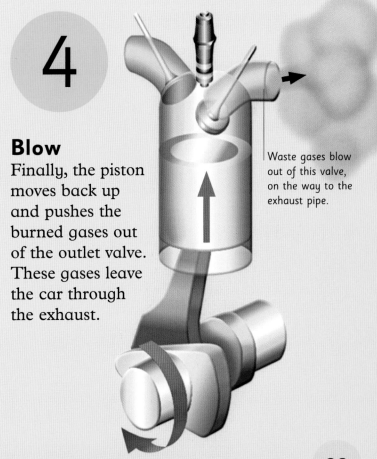

Blow

Finally, the piston moves back up and pushes the burned gases out of the outlet valve. These gases leave the car through the exhaust.

Waste gases blow out of this valve, on the way to the exhaust pipe.

It's a high-speed chemical reaction that produces heat and light.

Race cars

Formula 1 cars are like normal cars in many ways. They have gas engines, gears, and steering wheels. However, they are built with only one thing in mind, and that's WINNING RACES!

A technical masterpiece

Every bit of a Formula 1 (F1) car is light and very strong. At its peak speed of 225 mph (360 kph), air flows over it with the force of a tornado, so it is built to be as low and streamlined as possible.

Pit stop pressure

At pit stops, a driver refuels and gets new tires. This is all done in about 30 seconds. That's about the same amount of time as it takes to read this paragraph!

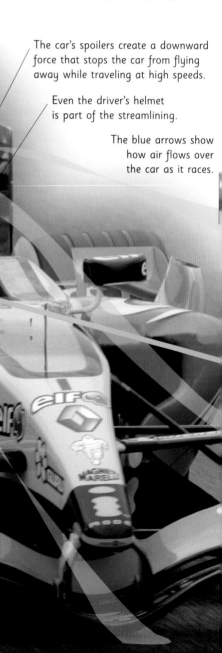

The car's spoilers create a downward force that stops the car from flying away while traveling at high speeds.

Even the driver's helmet is part of the streamlining.

The blue arrows show how air flows over the car as it races.

34

What is the minimum weight of Formula 1 race car?

G-force

While driving at super-high speeds, a Formula 1 driver experiences a pushing force called g-force, which can be up to six times more powerful than gravity. It can shove a driver backward, forward, and sideways as the car twists around the track. You can see g-force at work in a normal car by watching water sloshing in a cup.

This helmet is attached to the seat to stop the driver's head from swinging around because of g-force.

Inertia

G-force is caused by inertia. The law of inertia says that moving objects try to travel straight at a constant speed. When a car stops abruptly, your body tries to keep going forward.

The car accelerates

Water spills out backward.

The car brakes

Water spills out forward.

The car turns right

Water spills out to the left.

The car turns left

Water spills out to the right.

Steering wheel

Because an F1 driver is concentrating so hard on winning a race and because the inside of the car is so tight, all the controls for the car are close to the driver's hand on the steering wheel. There are only two foot pedals—the brake and the accelerator.

Buttons like these fulfil all an F1 driver needs, from traction control to drinks dispenser—drinks are pumped by tube straight into the driver's mouth.

35

Including the driver and excluding fuel, the minimum weight is 1,630 lb (740 kg).

Up to speed

Once you're on the move, you usually want to go as fast as you can. But what makes sports cars really fast and tankers really slow? Speed isn't just about raw power—other factors are at work.

Speed, velocity, and acceleration

You measure speed by dividing the distance traveled by the time it takes. Speed is not the same as velocity, which is a measure of how fast you are going in a particular direction. You feel acceleration when you pedal your bike really hard. Acceleration measures how quickly your velocity is changing.

Acceleration isn't just speeding up. Scientists also use it to describe all changes in velocity, like slowing down and even changing direction.

Horsepower?

Engine power is still measured using a very old unit—the horsepower. It is based on how many horses would be needed to provide the same amount of pulling power. The average car engine has around 135 horsepower.

How fast are electric cars?

Pulling power

If you have a powerful engine, you can accelerate very fast, which is why a sports car will always beat a lawnmower. But if you give a lift to an elephant, your acceleration will suffer. That is because it takes more force to speed up heavy objects.

Milk tanker vs. Ariel Atom

Both have a 300 horsepower engine. A full tanker can weigh as much as 100 tons (110 metric tons). The Atom weighs half a ton (0.55 metric tons). Even though they have the same pulling power, the weight of the milk means the tanker takes 35 seconds to accelerate from 0 to 60 mph (0 to 97 kph). The Atom can do it in 2.7 seconds, making it one of the fastest accelerating road cars in the world.

Not such a drag

No vehicle ever made can accelerate as fast as a drag racing car, or dragster. They can go from 0 to 330 mph (0 to 531 kph) in less than 4.5 seconds. Dragsters use nitromethane as fuel, which provides twice as much power as gas. The rear wheels have to be really big to transfer the high power made by the engine.

Superfast cars

If you want to go really fast and break records, then there's only one solution—strap a jet engine or two to your chassis. Jet engines don't use pistons. Instead, they suck air through the front of the engine, use it to burn fuel, and then blast the hot exhaust out of the back. This pushes the car forward at speeds of up to 760 mph (1,223 kph).

The Tesla Roadster can reach a speed of 130 mph (209 kph).

Powering up

Most cars are powered by gasoline engines, but there are many other ways to power a vehicle. Today, renewable forms of energy that don't depend on fossil fuels such as gas are being used more widely.

Electric car

Electric cars use rechargeable batteries instead of gas. The batteries release energy in the form of electricity, which drives a motor that runs the car. While it is easy to charge such cars, it can take hours.

Solar car

The solar panels on a solar car use sunlight to generate electricity. The electricity powers an electric motor that turns the wheels. Solar cars are not powerful, and so are usually very light and streamlined.

Solar cars work best in very sunny places. They tend to be flat, and very wide or long to create room for the large solar panels on the roof.

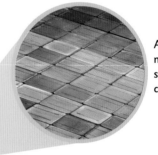

A solar panel is made of lots of separate units called cells.

The curved front and flat body make the car streamlined, which reduces the energy it needs to run smoothly.

When did the hybrid car go on sale?

Biofuel

Many ordinary cars can run on biofuels—fuels made from plants. Biodiesel, for instance, is a biofuel made from vegetable oil. In some countries, including Brazil and the US, gas is diluted with alcohol made from corn or sugarcane. Using biofuels reduces pollution, but this can harm the environment—vast areas of land are used up to produce these fuels.

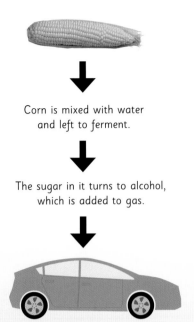

Corn is mixed with water and left to ferment.

The sugar in it turns to alcohol, which is added to gas.

Hydrogen power

Hydrogen-powered vehicles use liquid hydrogen as a fuel. The hydrogen flows into a device called a fuel cell, which combines hydrogen with oxygen from the air to make water and electricity. The electricity drives the car's motor and wheels, just as in an electric car. The water is released as exhaust.

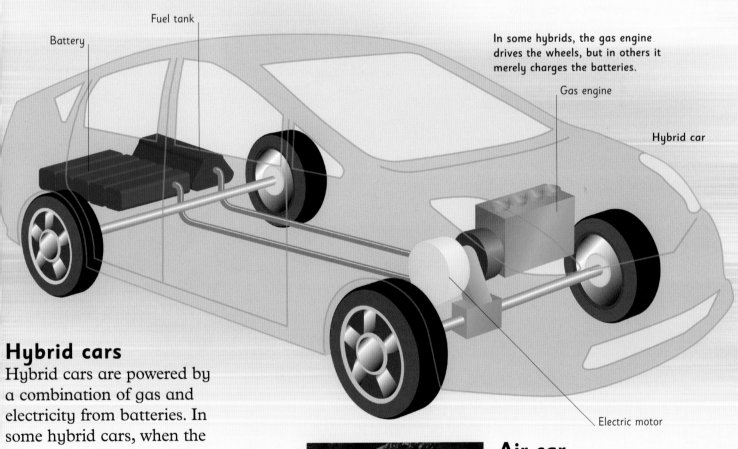

Fuel tank

Battery

In some hybrids, the gas engine drives the wheels, but in others it merely charges the batteries.

Gas engine

Hybrid car

Electric motor

Hybrid cars

Hybrid cars are powered by a combination of gas and electricity from batteries. In some hybrid cars, when the car stops, the brakes capture the energy released and use it to charge the batteries. A computer switches between the two forms of power to make the best use of energy.

Air car

The air car works a bit like a balloon. High-pressure air is stored in an air tank. When the driver pushes the accelerator pedal, the air is released through a valve. This jet of air turns the engine.

In 1917.

Trains and tracks

Most countries have a railroad system where trains travel on steel tracks. Trains are often powered by electricity that runs through rails or overhead wires.

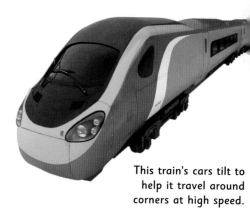

This train's cars tilt to help it travel around corners at high speed.

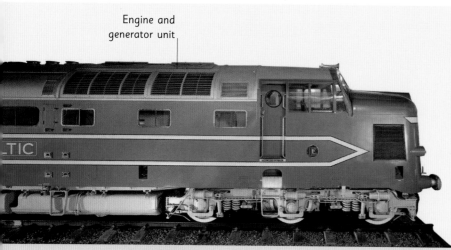

Engine and generator unit

Diesel electric

Some electric trains run on diesel fuel. The diesel is burned to make electricity. This electricity powers the motors that make the wheels turn and the train move.

Most freight trains are fueled by diesel.

Electric third rail

Several trains use an electrified third rail. The train picks up the electricity using a device called a shoe.

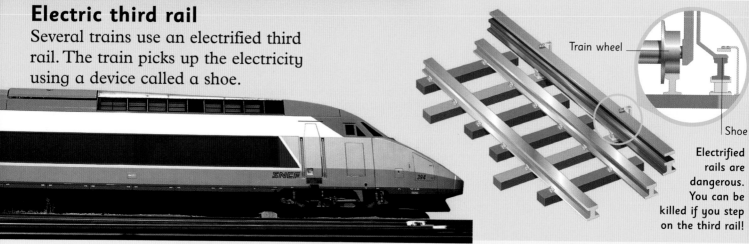

Train wheel

Shoe

Electrified rails are dangerous. You can be killed if you step on the third rail!

Overhead wires

There are trains that draw electricity from overhead wires using a metal arm. The cables carry high-voltage electricity—around 25,000 volts.

The train's metal arm is called a pantograph.

What is a maglev train?

Signals

Signals tell the train engineer when it is safe to move forward, when to proceed to the next section of track, and when to stop. Signals use red-, yellow-, and green-colored lights, just like traffic lights.

You need wheels

Trains have metal wheels with a rim, called a flange, on the inside to stop them from slipping off the track. Usually the flanges never touch the rails, but if they do, you hear a squealing noise.

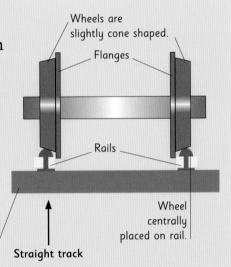

Wheels are slightly cone shaped.

Flanges

Rails

A tie is a block that supports the rails and holds them in place.

Straight track

Wheel centrally placed on rail.

On the tracks

Railroad tracks guide trains from station to station. They are made of steel and usually welded together to give a smooth ride. Some rails are moveable. These are called points. They help the train switch from one track to another.

A ◄━━━━━━━━━━━━━━━━━━━━ B

Points

C

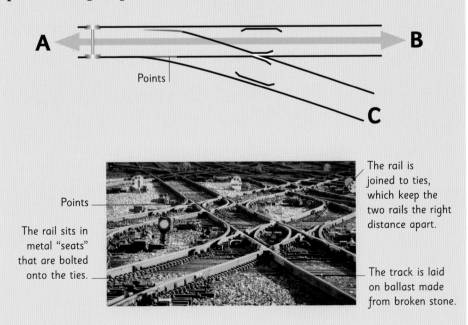

Points

The rail sits in metal "seats" that are bolted onto the ties.

The rail is joined to ties, which keep the two rails the right distance apart.

The track is laid on ballast made from broken stone.

Train travel

Trains can transport a large number of people and goods efficiently across long distances.

Freight trains carry goods and can be more than 2 miles (3.5 km) long.

Bullet trains in Japan are the world's first high-speed rail service.

The French TGV is the fastest train ever built. It can go at 357 mph (575 kph).

Eurostar travels between England and France through the Channel Tunnel, which runs under water.

The Trans-Siberian Express makes the longest journey— 5,857 miles (9,297 km).

The Qinghai–Tibet railroad is the world's highest—passengers need to carry oxygen.

Braking on ice

Metal wheels can slip when the engineer brakes on icy rails. So a small amount of sand is dropped in front of them to help them grip the rail.

A train that uses electromagnetism to lift it off the ground and move forward.

Gases and liquids

Air and water are important examples of two types of substance—gases and liquids. They behave in different ways.

What's a molecule?

Liquids and gases are made of molecules. Molecules are so tiny you can't see them with the naked eye. Molecules are made of even tinier particles called atoms. Everything in the universe is made of atoms.

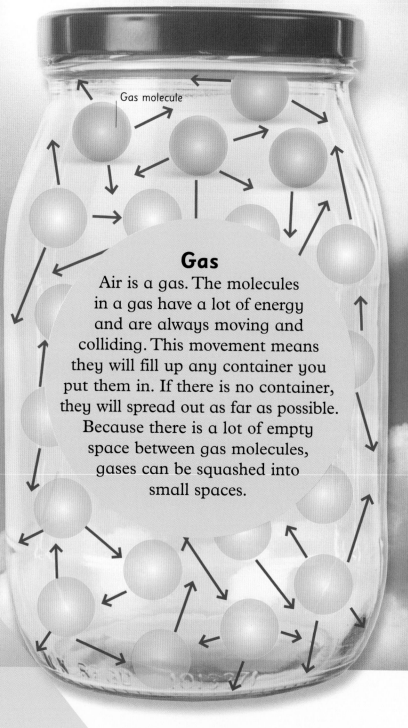

Gas molecule

Gas

Air is a gas. The molecules in a gas have a lot of energy and are always moving and colliding. This movement means they will fill up any container you put them in. If there is no container, they will spread out as far as possible. Because there is a lot of empty space between gas molecules, gases can be squashed into small spaces.

Feel the breeze

You can feel air molecules moving when the wind blows. Wind is simply air molecules being pushed by a force we call pressure.

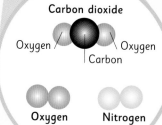

Carbon dioxide

Oxygen   Oxygen

Carbon

Oxygen   Nitrogen

Air molecules

Air is made up of lots of different atoms bonded together in units called molecules. The main molecules in air are nitrogen, oxygen, and carbon dioxide.

What do we call materials in which the atoms do not move around?

Scientists call water molecules H₂O (H stands for hydrogen and O stands for oxygen).

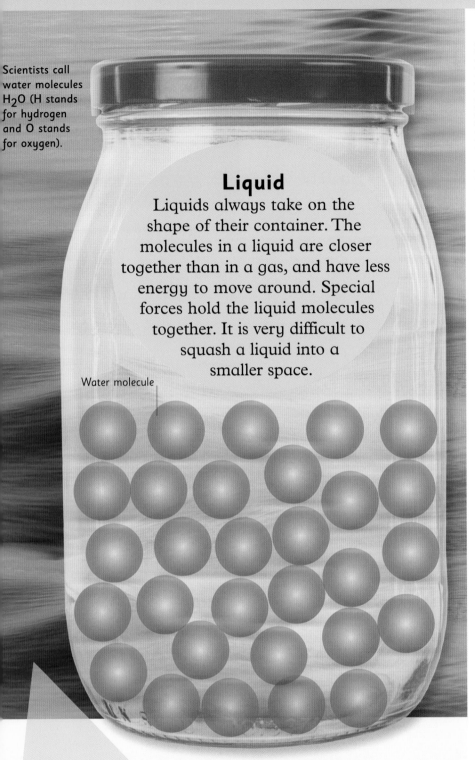

Liquid
Liquids always take on the shape of their container. The molecules in a liquid are closer together than in a gas, and have less energy to move around. Special forces hold the liquid molecules together. It is very difficult to squash a liquid into a smaller space.

Water molecule

Water molecules
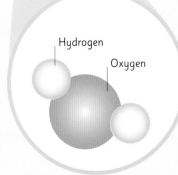

Water molecules are made of two hydrogen atoms bonded to one oxygen atom. Water molecules are so sticky, they clump together to form drops.

Hydrogen

Oxygen

Picture detective
Look through the Gases and liquids pages and see if you can identify the picture clues below.

Turn and learn
How ships float:
pp. 46–47
How airplanes fly:
pp. 52–53

43

Solids—the atoms in a solid only vibrate in a fixed position.

How fluids work

Gases, such as air, and liquids, such as water, are known as "fluids." This is because they move in a similar way and can flow around corners and fill containers.

Streamlined car
A car is designed to be as streamlined as possible, so air can pass smoothly over it.

Fluid motion
Fluids flow smoothly over curved (streamlined) objects. They do not flow smoothly over shapes that have corners and bumps. These slow fluids down, causing a force called drag.

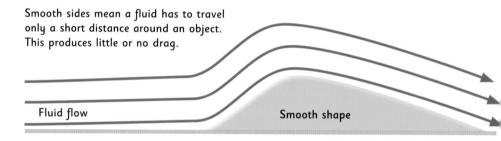

Smooth sides mean a fluid has to travel only a short distance around an object. This produces little or no drag.

Fluid flow

Smooth shape

Block shapes with flat edges split the fluid's flow into different streams. Some pass over an object. Some pass around it. Others twist and turn back, creating areas of drag known as eddies.

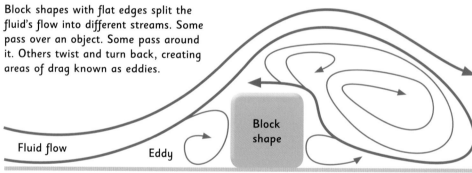

Fluid flow

Eddy

Block shape

Sir Isaac Newton discovered gravity when an apple fell from a tree.

Gravity and weight
Gravity is the force that keeps you stuck to the ground. It also keeps the moon in orbit around the Earth, and keeps the Earth traveling around the sun. Gravity is what gives you weight. Without your weight pulling you downward, you would simply float away as if you were in space.

What is denser—water or air?

How dense?

The weight of an object depends upon its mass—the amount of matter it's made of. Matter is made of atoms. Substances in which the atoms are heavy and closely packed are said to be more "dense" than substances whose atoms are lighter, and less closely packed.

A pound of bricks weighs the same as a pound of oranges, but the oranges take up more space. The mass of the bricks is packed into a smaller space, so we say the bricks have a higher density than the oranges.

Floating and sinking

An object that is free to move in a fluid will either float or sink, depending on its density and the density of the fluid.

An object will **float** in air if it is **less dense** than air.

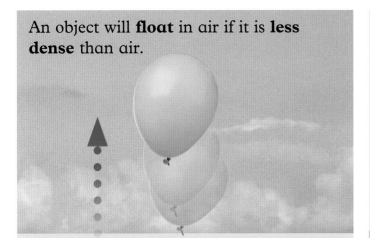

The gas inside the balloon is less dense than the air around it, so it slowly rises.

An object will **float** in water if it is **less dense** than water.

Boats float because they are mainly filled with air, which is less dense than water.

An object will **sink** in air if it is **more dense** than air.

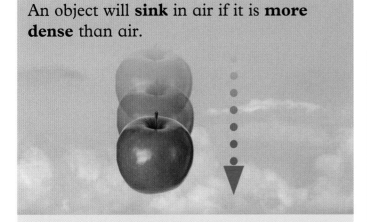

Apples are denser than air so they drop from trees.

An object will **sink** in water if it is **more dense** than water.

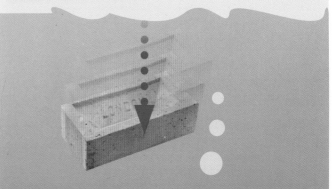

Brick molecules are very close together, making bricks dense, and so they sink.

Water has 1,000 times the density of air.

Float that boat

How do ships float, and why do they sometimes sink? It's all to do with buoyancy.

Setting sail

A ship is very heavy, especially when it's loaded with crew, passengers, and cargo. But the ship still floats because as it pushes down, it displaces water, and the displaced water pushes upward. If the ship weighs less than the displaced water, it will float (see p. 45).

Floating beach ball

Buoyancy

When an object weighs less than the amount of water it displaces, it floats, or is "buoyant." If it weighs more, it sinks.

Sinking golf ball

The weight of the ship is spread out across the hull.

Gravity

Buoyancy

Balancing act

While buoyancy pushes the boat upward, gravity pulls it downward. These two forces balance each other out, so a ship can float on the water.

46

Safety systems

A ship may sink if it takes on water. To help prevent this, ships have safety features such as bulkheads. If one compartment starts to leak, the bulkheads stop the water flooding the whole ship.

Bulkheads are walls that divide large areas into smaller ones in a ship.

Bulkheads

Double hull

A big ship usually has a double hull, which is like a tire with an inner tube. It gives extra protection if the ship collides with rocks or icebergs.

Hull   Double hull

The steel hull is full of air, which is very light and keeps the ship afloat.

That sinking feeling

The air inside a ship's hull makes the ship less dense than the water around it. If the ship hits a rock and rips a hole in its hull, water pours in and replaces the air. This makes the ship denser and it sinks.

This ship is taking on water and has started to sink.

Going down

Submarines are not like other boats—they have to be able to sink or float on command. They do this by filling and emptying their ballast tanks with air or water.

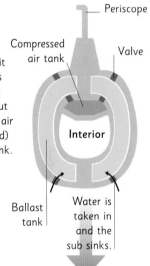

1 The weight of a submarine's hull helps it to go underwater, but it can't sink when there is air in the ballast tanks. Most of the air is let out through a valve. Some air is compressed (squashed) into a small holding tank. Water is then pumped into the tanks and the sub sinks.

Periscope

Compressed air tank

Valve

Interior

Ballast tank

Water is taken in and the sub sinks.

Air flows into the ballast tanks.

2 When the sub is underwater, air is pumped back into the ballast tanks until the density of the sub matches that of the water around it. The sub can stay at one level as it moves through the water.

Water is forced out.

3 When it's time to surface, more air is pumped into the tanks, pushing out the water. Once it's at the surface, air is sucked in to fill the ballast tanks and the sub floats.

Air fills the tanks and the sub rises.

Water is forced out.

A ship called *Pioneering Spirit*. It is 1,253 ft (382 m) long and 407 ft (124 m) wide.

Floating balloons

Why do some balloons rise up into the air while others drop to the floor? To understand this, you have to look at the gases inside them.

An airship can rise to more than 6,500 ft (2,000 m). By comparison, a passenger jet normally cruises at around 30,000 ft (10,000 m).

Party balloons are filled with helium gas.

Helium
This balloon is filled with a gas called helium. Helium is less dense than air, so this balloon floats.

At parties, helium balloons are tied down so they don't float away!

Heavy air
When a balloon is filled with a gas that is less dense than air, it floats. When it is filled with a gas that is denser than air, it sinks.

Carbon dioxide
When you blow up a balloon with your breath, the air inside contains more carbon dioxide than the air outside. It is also under more pressure. As a result, the air inside the balloon is denser than the surrounding air, causing the balloon to sink.

Helium facts

Helium gas has no smell. It makes up about seven percent of natural gas.

Deep-sea divers breathe in a mixture of helium and oxygen.

Helium boils at a very low temperature—-452 °F (-233 °C) and turns to gas.

Helium, found in stars, is named after the Greek word for the sun—helios.

Liquid helium is colorless and very cold. It helps launch space rockets.

What is the only element to be discovered in space before it was found on the Earth?

Flying ships of air

An airship is known as a lighter-than-air (LTA) craft. Airships have a main, helium-filled balloon and two other large internal balloons, called ballonets. To control how high an airship floats, the ballonets take in or release air.

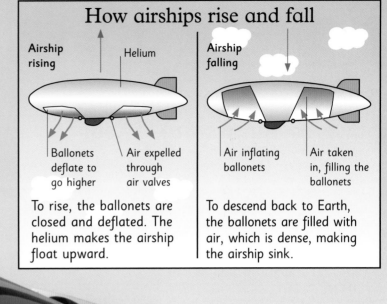

How airships rise and fall

Airship rising — Helium

Ballonets deflate to go higher | Air expelled through air valves

To rise, the ballonets are closed and deflated. The helium makes the airship float upward.

Airship falling

Air inflating ballonets | Air taken in, filling the ballonets

To descend back to Earth, the ballonets are filled with air, which is dense, making the airship sink.

RIQUEST

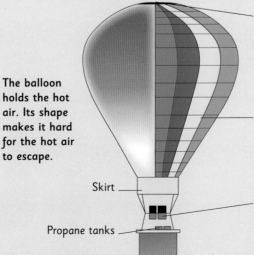

How hot-air balloons work

Hot-air balloons float upward when the air inside them is heated. This gives the air molecules more energy and they move farther apart, which makes the air less dense.

The balloon holds the hot air. Its shape makes it hard for the hot air to escape.

A flap at the top of the balloon allows hot air to escape and controls how quickly the balloon sinks.

Fabric panels are sewn together sideways and lengthwise to give the balloon strength.

Skirt

Propane tanks

Burners use propane gas to produce a hot flame, which heats the air inside the balloon.

 Cold air weighs more because its molecules are closer together.

 Hot air is less dense because its molecules are farther apart.

Roller coaster

These rip-roaring rides are powered by gravity. They slingshot thrill-seeking passengers along at breathtaking speeds.

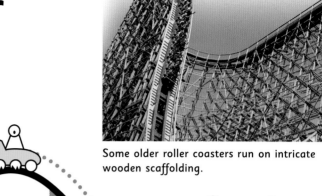

Some older roller coasters run on intricate wooden scaffolding.

Going up...

As the roller coaster goes up the first, tallest hill (called the lift hill), it's gradually building up potential energy (the energy stored in an object as a result of its position).

There is maximum potential energy at the top of the hill.

Over the top

At the top of a hill, coaster cars have high potential energy. This becomes kinetic energy (the energy of motion) as the coaster rolls down the slope

The cars gain speed as they roll down the hill.

Rushing down a steep slope can make you feel almost weightless, which may be very uncomfortable!

Chain reaction

Roller coaster cars don't have motors. They're pulled to the top of the first hill by a chain connected to a motor at the top.

blue fire

Where was the world's first roller coaster?

Wheeeeeeee!

Lots of different things affect the way you feel when you're rushing around a roller coaster.

→ Pushing against seat

→ Seat pushing back on you

→ Weight (gravity)

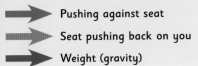

Shoulder harness

Bendable metal

The tracks and supports of most roller coasters are made from hollow steel. This can be shaped into loops and corkscrews.

Safety first

All riders are protected by a safety harness. Brakes are built into the track, not the cars. These are used at the end of the ride, or in emergencies.

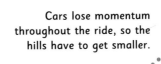

At the bottom of a loop your seat pushes against you as you push down on it, making you feel heavy. At the top, gravity pulls you away from your seat, so you feel weightless.

There is maximum kinetic energy at the bottom of the hill.

Cars lose momentum throughout the ride, so the hills have to get smaller.

Staying on track

Roller coaster cars are clamped securely to the rails by three sets of wheels. Load wheels sit on top of the tracks, upstop wheels run along the bottom of the tracks, and guide wheels run along the sides.

— Steel track

— Load wheels

— Guide wheels

— Upstop wheels

Ultimate experience

Thrill seekers in Florida can enjoy the Rip Ride Rockit roller coaster. It's very short and powerful, so it can pivot like a skateboard and climb straight uphill.

Passengers can choose the music they hear while they're terrified.

The very first roller coaster was an elaborate ice slide built in Russia during the 1600s.

How do planes fly?

Huge, heavy machines seem to defy gravity by staying up in the air! Yet airplanes fly around the world every day. This is because they can create the forces needed to fly.

The forces of flight
There are four forces acting on airplanes: thrust, drag, lift, and weight. A pilot can change all of these except weight. In level flight at a constant speed, all four forces must balance.

Thrusting forward
Planes need to create thrust to move forward through the air. This plane has a propeller to create thrust. As the propeller turns, it draws air past the blades, which pulls the plane forward.

Thrust

Cockpit

Engine

Propeller

A bumpy ride
Just like boats bounce over waves, planes can bounce up and down in the air. This happens when pockets of air move at different speeds, creating "turbulence." It can be caused by strong winds, storms, or when cold and warm air meet.

Level of plane

Cooler air

Warmer air rises faster, "bumping" the plane upward.

The biggest jumbo
The world's largest plane is the Airbus A380. At 240 ft (73 m) long, this jumbo jet can carry up to 853 passengers. It's 10 times longer than the four-seater Cessna 400.

Cessna 400

Airbus A380

What was the first airplane to stay in the air successfully?

As the plane moves, the wing divides the air, creating an area of low pressure above the wing and an area of higher pressure below it.

Lifting up
Lift is the opposite force to weight. A plane creates most of its lift with its wings.

Lift

Airflow

The difference in air pressure below and above the wing is what creates lift—the force that makes the airplane fly.

Aileron

Tail fin

Fuselage

Elevator / Rudder

Wing / Flap

Weight

Weighing down
Weight is caused by gravity pulling down on an object. Everything has weight, even air.

Drag

Dragging back
Drag is the opposite force to thrust—it slows down things. Imagine trailing your hand in water as you sail along in a boat. You can feel the water push back, or drag, against your hand. Air has the same effect on planes (and anything else that moves). A plane's smooth surface and streamlined shape help reduce drag.

What does that bit do?
Every part of a plane has a job to do, from the streamlined nose to the tail fin that keeps the plane steady in the sky.

Flaps that come down from the wings are used to increase lift during takeoff and landing.

Ailerons on the back edge of the wings are used to "roll" the plane, to make it turn or keep it level.

A rudder in the plane's tail turns the plane left or right.

Elevators in the tail move up and down to balance the position of the nose, keeping the plane level.

53

Nose cone

Soyuz spacecraft (inside casing)

Third stage

Second stage

First stage
(booster rockets)

Thrust

Gravity

Blast off!

Space is the final frontier. So far, we have explored only a tiny part of our galaxy, and this has been very difficult, dangerous, and expensive to do.

What makes rockets go?

Most rockets need two different chemicals—a fuel and an oxidizer. When they're mixed together, they cause a fierce but smooth burn—this is funneled downward, propelling the rocket upward. Clamps hold it down while the power builds, so it doesn't go head over tail and crash. At the words "blast off", the clamps are removed and the rocket is on its way. The rocket shown here is a Soyuz rocket. It takes people to the International Space Station (ISS).

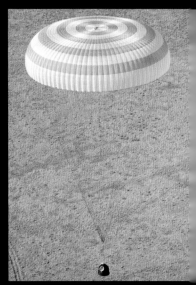

The Soyuz descent module slows down as it falls through Earth's atmosphere, and a parachute slows it even more, so that the astronauts inside can land safely.

When was the first liquid-fueled rocket made?

Space journey

After rockets are launched, they use huge amounts of fuel to get into Earth's orbit. The Soyuz rocket is made of different parts, or "stages." As one stage runs out of fuel, it falls away so that the rest of the rocket does not have to carry its weight.

The ISS is a laboratory in space used for scientific research. It orbits the Earth at an altitude of 250 miles (400 km).

Orbit

2 First stage (booster rockets) falls away.

3 Second stage falls away and spacecraft casing falls off.

4 Third stage falls away and spacecraft enters orbit.

1 Rocket blasts off from launchpad.

5 Soyuz spacecraft docks with ISS.

6 Soyuz spacecraft separates from ISS.

Descent module parachutes to ground.

8

Space junk

Experts believe there are more than 300,000 objects orbiting the Earth— pieces from satellites, bags of trash, and dropped tools.

7 Spacecraft separates into orbital, service, and descent modules.

55

In March 1926, by Dr. Robert H. Goddard in Massachusetts.

What is energy?

Energy is what makes everything happen. It is involved in every action we make. It powers your muscles, runs your car, and lights your home. Without energy you could not ride a bike, watch television, or fly in an airplane.

Different types of energy

Energy can't be made or destroyed. It just changes from one type to another. Here are some of the main types of energy.

Light

It is a form of energy we can see. Like X-rays and radio waves, it is also electromagnetic energy. It travels at an extremely high speed.

Internal energy

It is the energy of atoms or molecules vibrating. The hotter an object is, the faster the particles move. A transfer of internal energy is called heat.

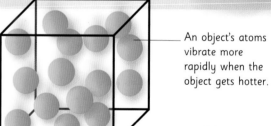

An object's atoms vibrate more rapidly when the object gets hotter.

Nuclear energy

It is stored in atoms. Nuclear energy is used to run power plants that generate electricity.

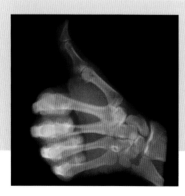

Electromagnetic energy

It is carried by X-rays, radio waves, and microwaves.

How big is an atom?

Gravitational energy

It is the stored energy in an object that has been lifted but is not allowed to fall. Turbines in dams can turn gravitational energy into electrical energy.

Kinetic energy

It is the energy a moving object has. The faster a car moves, the more kinetic energy it has.

Electrical energy

Electrical energy can travel easily through wires. It is the energy we use to power devices in our homes.

Turn and learn
Power plants: **pp. 62–63**
Gravity: **pp. 44–45**

Picture detective

Look through the What is energy? pages and see if you can identify the picture clues below.

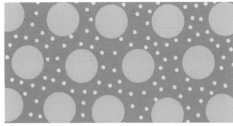

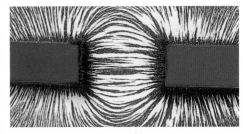

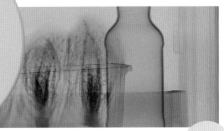

About 0.00000004 in (0.000001 mm) in diameter.

It's electric!

If you flip a switch to make something work, it probably runs on electricity. Most of the energy we use every day is electrical.

What is electricity?

Electricity is very convenient: It can power a huge range of devices—from lights to washing machines. Inside a metal wire, an electric current is simply the movement of tiny particles called electrons.

Starting small

Electrons are found in atoms—the particles of which everything is made. In metals, electrons are free from their atoms.

weird or what?

Inside the mains cables in your home, electrons move in one direction, and then the other, 60 times every second. This is called "alternating current".

Electricity passes freely from the socket to the lamp through the wiring.

Plugs have metal prongs that connect with the power supply wired into the wall.

BEWARE: ELECTRICAL CHARGE!

You should never put your finger or an object (other than a plug) into a socket—as you may get an electric shock.

Electrons carry an electrical charge.

Atom

Electrons

Flow of electricity

Electric current is simply the movement of electric charge. Electrons carry electric charge, and in a wire, the electrons are free to move.

When you turn on a lamp, electric current flows through the wire to the bulb, lighting it up.

58

imple circuit

An LED (light emitting diode) flashlight works using a imple electric circuit. Electric current flows from one nd of the batteries through the LED and back to the ther end of the batteries to complete the circuit.

hen the switch is in the ff" position, the circuit is oken and the LED does t light.

Electricity

When we talk about electricity, we use some important terms.

Conductors are materials that allow electricity to flow through them easily.

Circuits are paths that electric currents can flow along.

V **Voltage** is a measure of electrical strength.

A **Ampere** is a basic unit of electric current.

Current is the flow of electricity through a conductor.

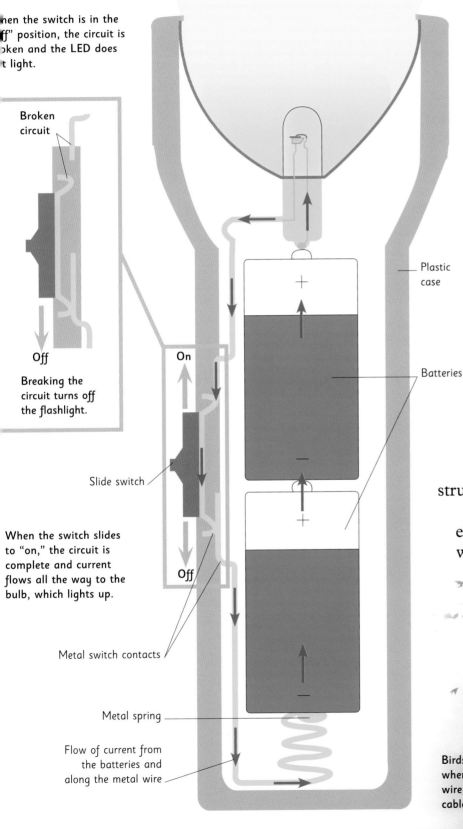

Broken circuit

Off

Breaking the circuit turns off the flashlight.

Plastic case

Batteries

On

Slide switch

When the switch slides to "on," the circuit is complete and current flows all the way to the bulb, which lights up.

Off

Metal switch contacts

Metal spring

Flow of current from the batteries and along the metal wire

Power towers

Electricity travels from power plants along thick cables, often strung between big metal towers. The cables carry very high voltages of electricity—enough to kill a person who comes into contact with them.

Birds don't complete a circuit when they sit on an electric wire, so they can perch on cables without being harmed.

An Italian named Alessandro Volta made the first battery in 1800.

The power of magnets

Magnets create an invisible force known as magnetism that repels and attracts certain substances, such as iron. Electricity and magnetism have a close relationship.

Can you field the force?

A magnetic field is the space around a magnet where its force can be felt. The field is strongest at the poles, and becomes weaker with increasing distance.

Iron filings reveal the magnetic field around a magnet

Poles

N   S   N   S

Opposite poles attract

Magnetic Earth

The Earth's central core has a strong magnetic field—it acts as a huge magnet. Its poles are close to the actual North and South Poles. Although they aren't in the same place as the geographical poles, they are very close. Over the Earth's lifetime, the magnetic poles have switched around a few times.

S   S

Similar poles repel

Magnets have two points where their field is strongest, known as poles. Each magnet has a north and south pole. These can attract and repel other magnets. Similar poles repel and opposites attract.

Super magnets

These are really strong magnets. They can be natural magnets or electromagnets.

The maglev train uses an electromagnet.

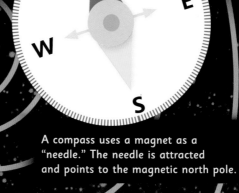

A compass uses a magnet as a "needle." The needle is attracted and points to the magnetic north pole.

Which elements are attracted to magnets?

Electromagnets

Electric currents produce magnetic fields—and magnetic fields can be used to produce electricity. An iron bar can become magnetic when an electric wire is wound around it in a coil. A moving magnet can also make an electric current in a coil of wire. Electromagnetic generators are used to create electricity at power plants.

Everyday magnets

Magnets are used in many everyday items, such as these.

 Audio speakers use electromagnets to make sound vibrations.

 Credit cards use a magnetic strip to store your information.

 Some handbags close with magnetic clasps.

 Central locking in a car uses a series of electromagnets to lock up.

Wheel power

A simple example of an electromagnetic generator is a bicycle dynamo. It uses the kinetic energy produced by the spinning wheel to turn the magnet past a coil of wire. The movement of the magnetic field produces enough electricity to light a bicycle light.

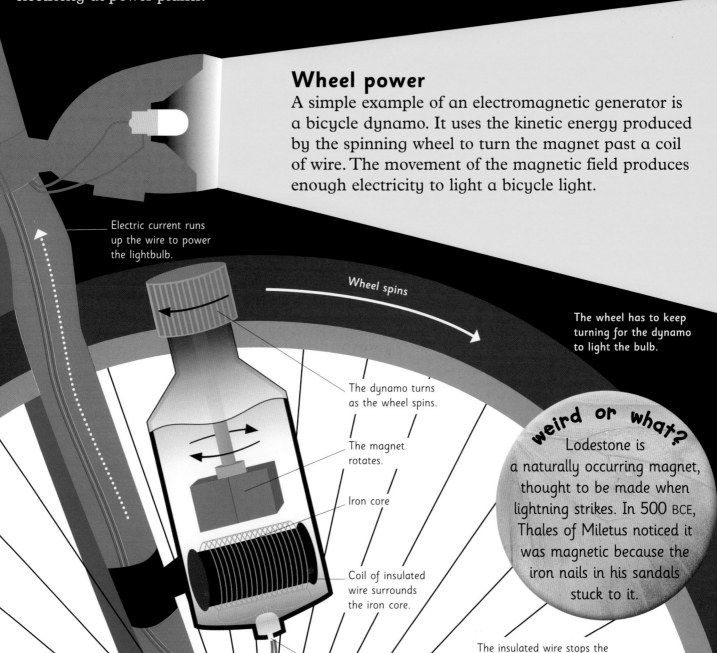

Electric current runs up the wire to power the lightbulb.

Wheel spins

The wheel has to keep turning for the dynamo to light the bulb.

The dynamo turns as the wheel spins.

The magnet rotates.

Iron core

Coil of insulated wire surrounds the iron core.

Electrical output

The insulated wire stops the current from taking a shortcut from loop to loop, and keeps it flowing around the core.

weird or what?
Lodestone is a naturally occurring magnet, thought to be made when lightning strikes. In 500 BCE, Thales of Miletus noticed it was magnetic because the iron nails in his sandals stuck to it.

Iron (Fe), nickel (Ni), and cobalt (Co) are all attracted to magnets.

Power plants

Most of the electricity that powers our homes, schools, factories, and businesses is generated in power plants. In most power plants, high-pressure steam turns huge machines called generators.

Vast quantities of coal being loaded onto a conveyor belt in Shanghai, China

Burn, burn, burn

Most power plants burn fossil fuels such as coal, oil, or natural gas. These are formed over millions of years as plant and plankton remains are subjected to heat and pressure. When fossil fuels are burned, they produce lots of heat, and lots of a gas called carbon dioxide.

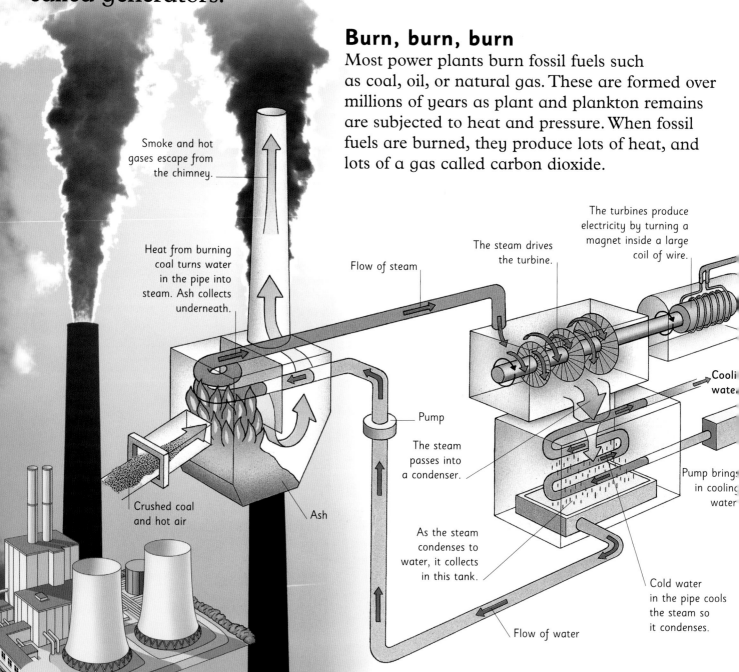

Smoke and hot gases escape from the chimney.

Heat from burning coal turns water in the pipe into steam. Ash collects underneath.

Crushed coal and hot air

Ash

Flow of steam

The steam drives the turbine.

The turbines produce electricity by turning a magnet inside a large coil of wire.

Pump

The steam passes into a condenser.

As the steam condenses to water, it collects in this tank.

Cooling water

Pump brings in cooling water

Cold water in the pipe cools the steam so it condenses.

Flow of water

62

Handle with care

Nuclear power plants create energy by splitting uranium atoms, which release heat. The heat boils water to produce steam, which powers the generators that make electricity. Spent nuclear fuel remains dangerously radioactive for thousands of years—and accidents can spread radioactivity into the environment.

On April 26, 1986, at 1:23 a.m., Reactor Four at Chernobyl Nuclear Power Plant in Ukraine exploded. Here, an inspector checks the reactor's deserted control room more than 20 years later.

Turn and learn
Renewable energy:
pp. 66–67

Green power

Burning fossil fuels harms the environment. There are less harmful energy sources that can be used to generate electricity.

 Solar power comes from the sun. In theory, it could provide all our energy.

 Hydroelectric power is generated by turbines turned by water falling through a dam.

 Wind power is generated by air flowing through wind turbines. Lots of turbines together make a wind farm.

 Tidal power uses the energy of the tides as seawater rises and falls.

 Biomass, such as wood chips, is made from plant matter, which releases energy when it is burned.

 Geothermal energy is heat from underground. Hot rocks are less deep in some places than others.

Transformer "steps up" the voltage.

Stretched between towers, cables carry electrical power across large distances.

Power towers are huge steel towers. They have extra wires running along the top to ground lightning.

Substations reduce voltage and send power in different directions.

Local grid

Electricity is wired to power points in your home. It connects with equipment through a plug.

On the way...

All over the world, rows of towers march across the landscape. They support the aluminum cables that carry electricity from power plants to homes and offices.

Cables below ground

Fossil fuels

Most of the energy we use comes from burning fossil fuels, but they won't last forever. Also, burning these fuels causes global warming, so it is important to use less energy and use other sources.

Saving energy
There are various ways in which you can save energy.

Grow your own fruit and vegetables. Try to eat food that is produced locally.

So you **don't waste heat**, ask your parents to make sure your home is insulated.

Save gas by walking when you can instead of asking for a ride.

Turn off your television and computer. Don't leave them on standby!

Turn off lights when you leave a room, and use energy-saving lightbulbs.

Dry laundry outside instead of using a dryer.

Oil and gas
We get oil by drilling under the ground—from dry land or the ocean floor. Today, oil makes up 33 percent of all energy use—for electricity generation, as fuel for heating, and as gasoline for cars. These uses release carbon dioxide and other pollutants into the air. Experts think oil reserves will eventually run out.

A drilling rig at sea extracts oil.

Coal energy
Excavated from the ground through deep mines or open pits, coal provides 40 percent of the energy for electricity generation. Coal was made long ago, and like other fossil fuels, new coal won't form quickly. Burning coal releases carbon into the air, resulting in pollution.

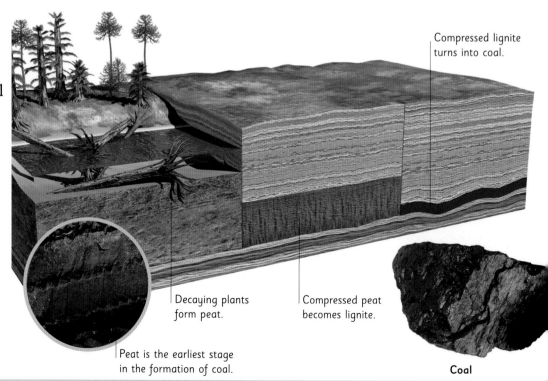

Compressed lignite turns into coal.

Decaying plants form peat.

Compressed peat becomes lignite.

Peat is the earliest stage in the formation of coal.

Coal

How much oil can the largest oil rig store?

Factories release a lot of carbon dioxide, which gets trapped inside our atmosphere.

Saving the Earth

When you reuse or recycle something, less energy is spent on making new products. So, less fossil fuel is used and fewer polluting gases are released. This is how recycling products, such as paper and plastic, can reduce global warning.

Universal symbol for recycling

It's getting hotter

Global warming is the gradual rise in the temperature of the Earth's atmosphere and surface. The atmosphere contains "greenhouse gases," which trap heat and keep the Earth warm. Burning fossil fuels releases extra greenhouse gases, making the Earth hotter. This harmful effect is called global warming.

Underground gas

Natural gas is also a fossil fuel. It comes from coal beds, marshes, bogs, and oil reserves. Although it is perhaps the cleanest fossil fuel, natural gas can easily leak into the atmosphere, adding to global warming. Natural gas is likely to run out in about 100 years. At the moment, it provides 22 percent of our energy.

This Gas Oil Separation Plant in Saudi Arabia burns off excess natural gas that cannot be sent to the refinery.

65

The Hibernia platform in the Atlantic Ocean can hold 1.3 million barrels of crude oil.

Renewable energy

Fossil fuels will eventually run out, but certain sources of energy are renewable, which means we can go on producing energy from them forever.

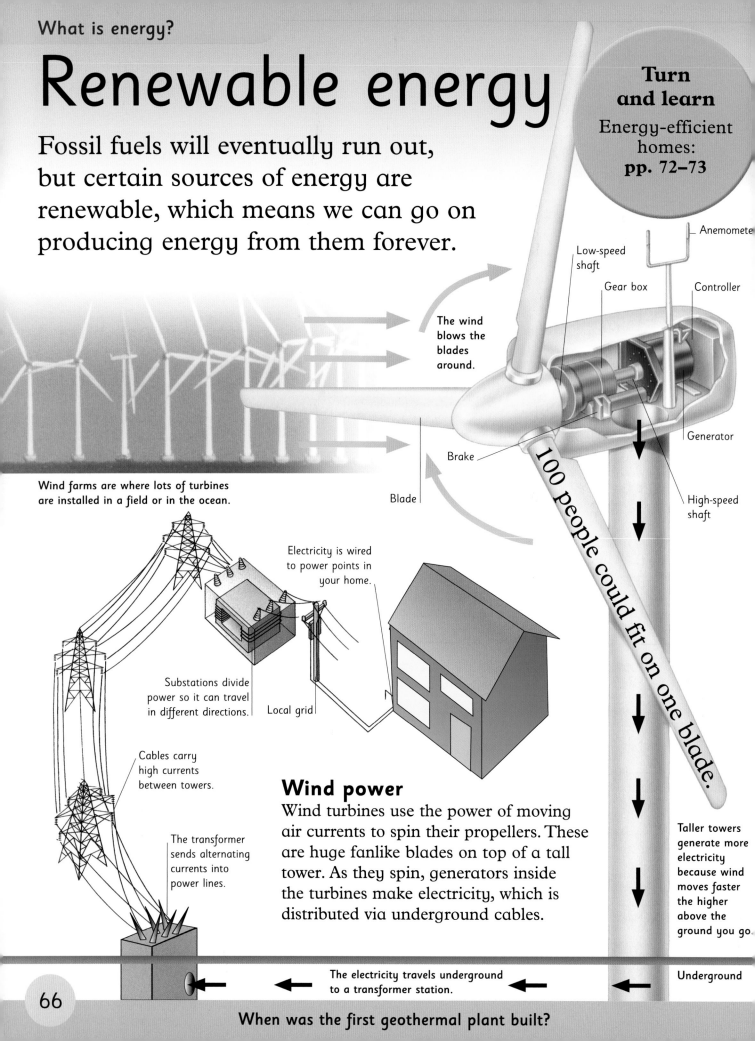

Turn and learn
Energy-efficient homes:
pp. 72–73

Anemometer

Low-speed shaft

Gear box

Controller

The wind blows the blades around.

Generator

Brake

High-speed shaft

Blade

Wind farms are where lots of turbines are installed in a field or in the ocean.

100 people could fit on one blade.

Electricity is wired to power points in your home.

Substations divide power so it can travel in different directions.

Local grid

Cables carry high currents between towers.

The transformer sends alternating currents into power lines.

Wind power

Wind turbines use the power of moving air currents to spin their propellers. These are huge fanlike blades on top of a tall tower. As they spin, generators inside the turbines make electricity, which is distributed via underground cables.

Taller towers generate more electricity because wind moves faster the higher above the ground you go.

The electricity travels underground to a transformer station.

Underground

When was the first geothermal plant built?

Hydroelectric power

A fifth of the world's electricity comes from hydroelectric power plants. Usually, a dam is built to trap a river and create a lake. The water is released at a controlled rate and allowed to flow through a spinning turbine, which drives an electricity generator.

The spillway of a dam is used to control the flow of water.

Water from a reservoir flows down a pipe to a turbine.

Electricity generator

Turbine

Solar energy

Huge panels are put on the roofs of buildings to capture energy from the sun and convert it into electricity. The stronger the sunlight, the more electricity they make.

When sunlight lands on a cell, electrons are pushed from one layer to the other, creating an electric current.

Solar panel

Photovoltaic cell

Pure silicon isn't a good conductor of electricity. Each cell contains silicon doped (made impure) with phosphorus, which produces free electrons.

Silicon mixed with boron makes "holes" where electrons are missing in the cell.

Geothermal energy

The Earth's crust is a hot place! Some rocks can be as hot as 1,800 °F (1,000 °C). Geothermal energy uses the heat from these rocks to generate electricity and heat water.

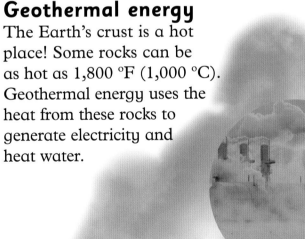

One of the biggest geothermal areas in the world is Iceland. People can swim next to this geothermal plant in Iceland since the water is so warm.

Biofuels

Biofuels come from fast-growing crops, such as corn, sugarcane, and palm oil. These fuels can add to or replace fossil fuels, such as diesel or gasoline. Biofuel production has been criticized for taking up land that could be used to grow food.

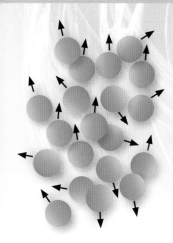

What's cooking?

The stove is probably the most important piece of equipment in the kitchen. Thanks to the stove, you don't have to eat your food raw.

The oven

Inside an electric oven are large coils of wire called heating elements. These get hot when electricity travels through them. They are controlled by a thermostat, which keeps the temperature inside constant.

Heat is a form of energy. It comes from the movement of atoms and molecules. The faster the molecules move around, the higher the temperature.

Dial controlling the thermostat

When the element inside the broiler gets hot, it loses heat through "heat radiation." The radiation travels in straight lines, heating everything in its path—including the food.

A hot element also heats the air that comes into contact with it. The air circulates inside the oven, heating the food. When the air gets too hot, the thermostat turns off the heating elements. It turns them back on again when the oven cools.

On a burner, the element is in direct contact with the saucepan, which passes the heat on to the food.

Some ovens have a fan that blows the air around and keeps the whole oven at the same temperature. Food cooks faster in a fan oven.

Can you put ice cream in an oven without melting it?

Heat's effect on food

Heating food makes the atoms and the molecules that make up the food jiggle around more rapidly. This extra energy is what causes changes to food.

Cooking eggs

Egg whites and yolks are made of long, stringy protein molecules dissolved in water.

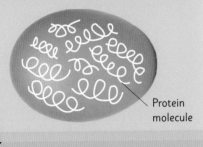

Protein molecule

Each individual molecule is twisted and curled up. When you add heat, the molecules uncurl and start to link together.

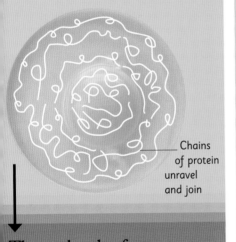

Chains of protein unravel and join

The molecules form a mesh that traps the water they floated in. The egg is now cooked.

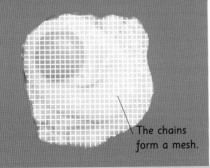

The chains form a mesh.

Baking bread

A bread mixture includes flour, water, and yeast. Yeast consists of millions of tiny organisms (fungi). Flour releases stretchy gluten when it mixes with water.

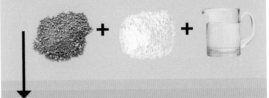

Yeast is inactive until it comes into contact with warm water. When the bread mix is left in a warm place, the yeast starts feeding on the sugars in the flour and releases carbon dioxide.

Gas is released

The gumlike gluten fills with thousands of gas bubbles, and the bread rises. Cooking traps the bubbles in the bread.

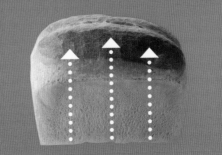

Sweet treats

Many candies are made by simply adding sugar to water and heating the mixture to very high temperatures.

As you cook it, the water boils away, leaving a much stronger solution of sugar. Very strong solutions make hard toffee or hard candy.

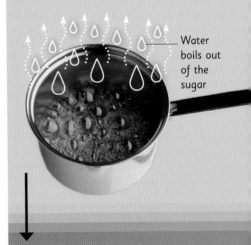

Water boils out of the sugar

If you stir the mixture as it cools, it forms crystals. This is how you make fudge. To make toffee, you leave it to set without stirring.

Yes, if you make baked Alaska—ice cream covered in meringue.

Keeping cool

We keep food cool so it stays fresh, and we keep liquids cool so they're refreshing to drink. Electricity makes all this possible.

Eggs are usually stored in the refrigerator door, which is a few degrees warmer than the shelves.

Lettuce and other salad vegetables go in the door or in a drawer at the bottom of the fridge.

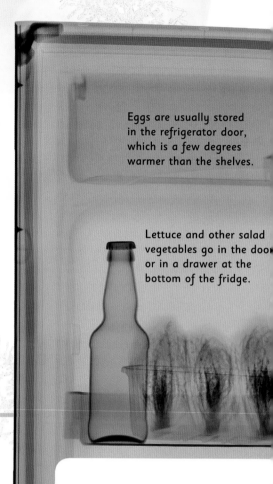

45 °F (7 °C) and above

Some foods don't need to be chilled to stay fresh.

Room temperature

Dry foods, such as beans and pasta, keep very well at room temperature. Root vegetables, such as potatoes, don't need refrigeration, but they keep best in a cool place rather than a warm one.

32–45 °F (0–7 °C)

Fridge

The temperature inside a refrigerator is cold enough to slow down the growth of bacteria (germs) in our food, so it stays fresh longer. Dairy products, meat, and fish should always be stored here.

Cool coil

A pump compresses refrigerant gases, heating and turning them into a liquid. The hot liquid evaporates, which cools it and turns it back into a gas. The cool gas absorbs heat as it passes through long coiled pipes set into the fridge walls.

Cold gas cools the fridge contents.

32 °F (0 °C) and below

Some treats and desserts are served frozen.

Freezer

Freezers are cold enough to make your skin freeze! Bacteria can't multiply in these temperatures, so food stays fresh for months or even years. Most foods are thawed or warmed before you eat them.

How quickly do bacteria grow at room temperature?

Adjustable
temperature control

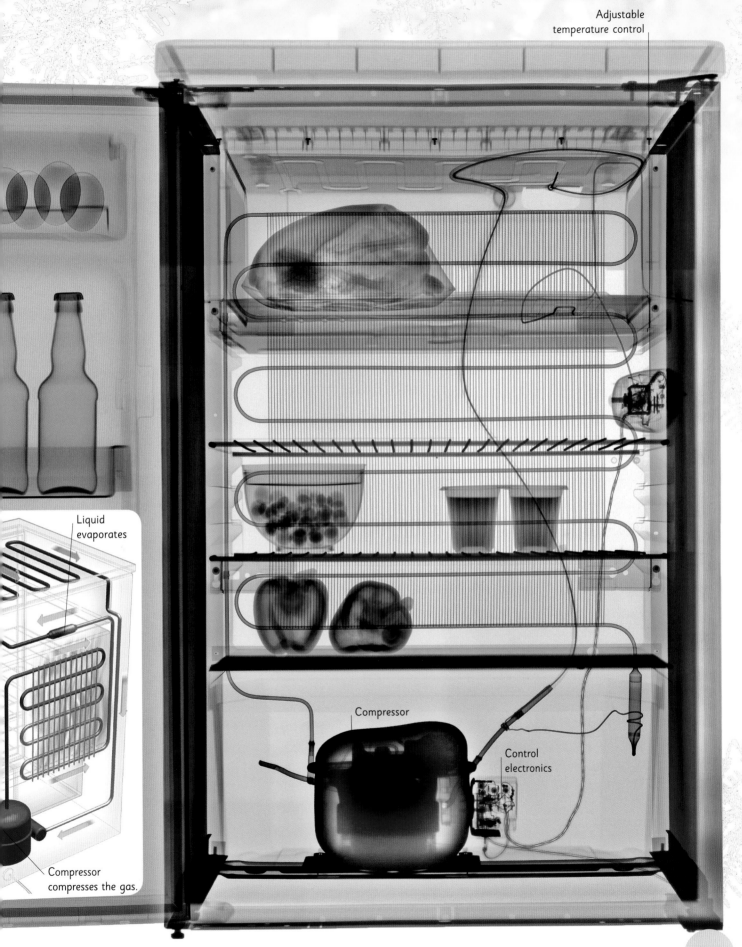

Compressor

Control
electronics

Liquid
evaporates

Compressor
compresses the gas.

In just four hours, one bacterium can turn into more than 1,000!

Energy efficiency

Every home needs energy, most of which comes from fossil fuels. It's important not to waste energy because fossil fuels will run out one day. Also, burning these fuels releases carbon dioxide into the air, adding to global warming.

Eco-living

Sustainable homes are designed to be better for the environment. They have lots of features that save energy and water. They produce fewer carbon emissions and are also cheaper to run.

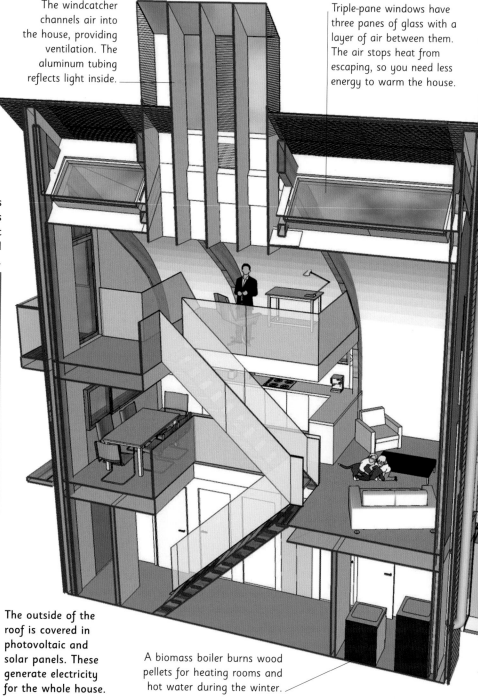

The windcatcher channels air into the house, providing ventilation. The aluminum tubing reflects light inside.

Triple-pane windows have three panes of glass with a layer of air between them. The air stops heat from escaping, so you need less energy to warm the house.

The "Lighthouse" is built with materials that absorb heat during the day and give it out at night.

The outside of the roof is covered in photovoltaic and solar panels. These generate electricity for the whole house.

A biomass boiler burns wood pellets for heating rooms and hot water during the winter.

72

In your home

We can all do things to make our homes more energy efficient. A lot of energy is used to heat a house. Ask your parents to insulate your attic to help keep in heat. You can also insulate walls and floors, plug gaps around doors and windows, and install storm windows.

Insulating an attic

Thermograms are pictures that show hot things as white and yellow, and cold things as blue. The hottest part of this house is its windows, because heat is escaping through them.

When rain hits the roof, it collects in a gutter and runs down a pipe into a recycling tank. The water is used in a washing machine.

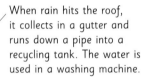

Turn and learn

Saving energy: **pp. 64–65**
Renewable energy: **pp. 66–67**

Batteries

Every household uses batteries to power all kinds of things—but batteries eventually run out. So how should you get rid of them?

Change old batteries right away. Batteries contain chemicals that may leak and ruin the gadget.

Don't throw your batteries in the trash. Recycle them instead—it's better for the environment.

Batteries should never be thrown onto a fire—they may explode.

When things break

However energy efficient you are, electrical goods will eventually need to be replaced. But some items are simply too dangerous to throw away. Old fridges contain gases that are harmful if they leak. The safest way to get rid of a broken fridge is to contact a disposal specialist to take it away.

Broken fridges must be carefully taken apart so they don't release harmful gases.

Make a difference

If you get a new computer or cell phone but there's nothing wrong with the old one, donate the old one to charity. Go online to find charities, schools, and groups that can make use of your unwanted equipment.

Gases containing carbon that are released into the air and may cause global warming.

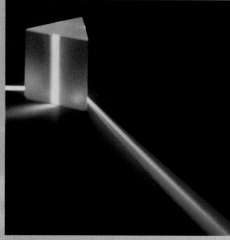
A glass prism splits light into colors.

Light and sound

We learn most of what we know about the world by seeing and hearing. We need light to be able to see, and sound around us to hear. Both reach us by traveling in waves.

White light

There is a range, or spectrum, of colors of light—from red to blue. When all the colors are mixed together, the result looks white. Sunlight is "white light"—but a glass prism will separate the colors. Each color bends at a different angle as the light passes through the prism, allowing us to see the individual colors.

The sun's atoms give out lots of light.

What is light?

Light is a type of energy called electromagnetic radiation. "Electromagnetic" means it's made up of electrical and magnetic energy, and "radiation" means it spreads out from a source. Electromagnetic radiation comes from particles that carry an electric charge—especially electrons in the atoms that make up everything around us.

The speed of light

Light travels in waves, a bit like waves that travel through water. It travels faster than anything else in the universe—an amazing 186,000 miles per second (300,000 km per second)! It takes just eight minutes for light from the sun to reach the Earth.

Light doesn't always behave like a wave. Sometimes it behaves like it's made up of particles, so it spreads out more like a spray of water from a hose than waves in the ocean.

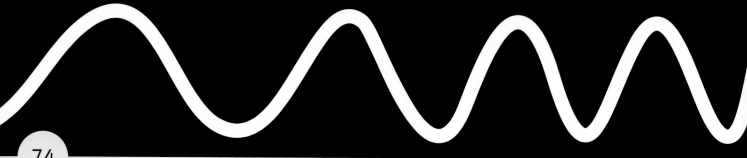

74

What is refraction?

Secrets of sound

When something vibrates, it squeezes and stretches the air around it, sending out waves that we hear as sound.

Echolocation

Some animals use sound to find their way around. This is called echolocation. Bats send out high-pitched squeaks that bounce off their surroundings. If their echo comes back quickly, it means there's something nearby.

Cymbals create large waves, which make a loud sound!

The speed of sound

Sound travels slower than light—about 1,220 ft per second (about 340 m per second) in air. Its speed changes depending on what the waves are traveling through. They can move four times faster in water than in air.

Picture detective

Look through the Light and sound pages and see if you can identify the picture clues below.

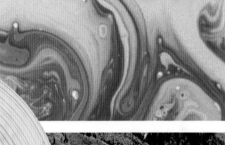

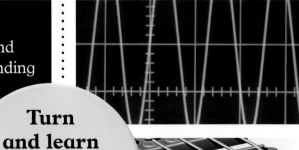

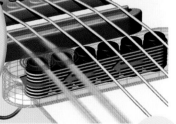

Turn and learn
Visible light:
pp. 76–77
How ears hear:
pp. 90–91

Refraction is when light waves bend, such as in a prism.

Now you see it...

Light waves (or electromagnetic waves) are all different lengths. The range of wavelengths we can see is called the visible spectrum. But there are other types of electromagnetic radiation, with longer or shorter wavelengths, that we cannot see.

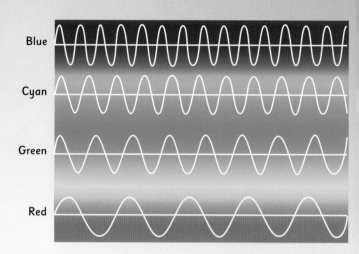

Blue
Cyan
Green
Red

... and now you don't

Our eyes can see only light waves of certain lengths—if they're longer or shorter, they're invisible. You may know some of the other forms of electromagnetic radiation, such as X-rays or microwaves. Although they are invisible, we make use of them every day.

Light of many colors

Visible light is made up of waves of different lengths. Each length appears as a separate color. For example, red waves are long and blue rays are short. Light contains an endless number of colors. The only limit is on how well your eye and brain can distinguish one wavelength from another.

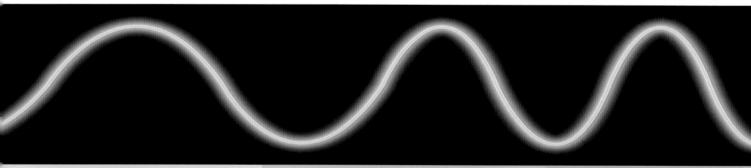

Radio waves

Radio waves carry sound and images through the air. Radios, televisions, and walkie-talkies all use radio waves. The longest radio waves can be 100,000 times longer than the shortest ones.

Microwaves

Microwaves are used to carry cell phone calls, and also to heat food in microwave ovens. Atoms in food absorb microwave energy and heat up. Some foods, such as those containing water, heat up more than others.

Infrared waves

Infrared waves carry heat. The waves can be seen through night-vision goggles or special cameras designed to detect heat rather than light. When you get near anything hot, you feel infrared rays.

76

Visible spectrum

I can see a rainbow

When it is raining and the sun is behind you, you may see a rainbow. Sunlight is a mixture of all the colors of visible light. Each color bends by a different amount as it enters a raindrop, bounces off the back, and bends again as it leaves. So you see a different color from each drop.

Colored or transparent

Some materials absorb some colors of light and reflect others, so they appear colored. Other materials are "transparent"—they let light pass through them.

A diamond is transparent. But light bends as it passes through it, like in a prism or a raindrop. It also bounces off the many faces inside and outside. The result is a sparkly effect, with colors and flashes of light.

Visible	Ultraviolet (UV) rays	X-rays	Gamma rays

  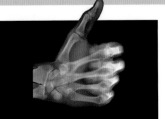 

Light sources, such as the sun, produce visible light. We see objects because visible light bounces off them.

Ultraviolet waves come straight from the sun. Some UV waves can burn your skin and, over time, cause wrinkles and cancer. That's why you should cover up and use sunscreen when you go outside in the sunlight.

X-ray waves pass through most things, but not bones, teeth, or metal. When doctors want to look at your bones, they take X-ray pictures.

Gamma rays can bore through solid objects and kill living cells. Doctors use them in radiotherapy to destroy cancer cells. Gamma rays are also released when nuclear bombs explode.

All the colors of visible light appearing together.

Light and bubbles

When light hits the surface of a bubble, it reflects off both the outside and the inside of its skin, producing the effect of swirling, shimmering colors.

Bubble colors

Bubbles are formed when air is trapped inside a thin layer of soapy water. You can see its colors when light waves reflect from the layer's outer and inner surfaces back to your eyes. The thickness of the bubble determines the the kind of colors you see. As some parts of the bubble are thicker than others, you see many colors at once.

These bubbles are on the surface of a soap-and-water solution

hands on

Make your own bubble solution by mixing half a cup of dish soap with four cups of water and four tablespoons of glycerine.

Color secrets

The colors you see on a bubble change as it gets thinner due to evaporation. In fact, you can tell how thick a bubble is by the colors it reflects. The blue parts of bubbles are thickest and the black parts are thinnest. Bubbles start to turn black when they are about to burst.

What happens when you blow soap bubbles in cold weather?

Tiny planets

The patterns on a bubble look a little like the patterns of clouds around a planet. Both are films of fluid, so they act in a similar way. This is why some scientists use bubbles as model planets—they study the surface patterns to discover how storms and hurricanes develop.

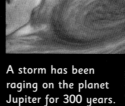

The colors on the surface of a soap bubble appear to swirl around like a storm on a planet.

A storm has been raging on the planet Jupiter for 300 years.

Bubble shapes

The water molecules in bubble solution hold tightly to one another, constantly pulling together. This means that bubbles always take up the smallest surface area possible.

When soap solution is stretched across a bubble wand, the smallest surface it can form is a flat plane.

When the solution is stretched around a pocket of air, the smallest surface it can make is a ball.

If two bubbles meet in midair, they shrink their surface area by forming a shared, flat wall between them.

When three bubbles meet, they share three walls. The point at which these walls meet always measures 120 degrees.

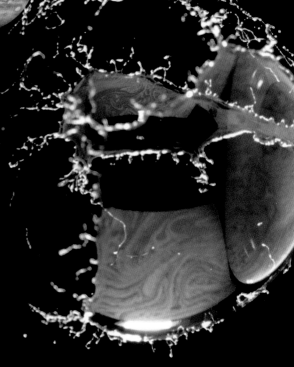

Bursting bubbles

Soap bubbles burst when they touch anything that's dry (such as a finger), or when the water in them evaporates.

The water in them turns to ice—so they freeze.

Mirror, roяяiM

When you want to see yourself, you look in a mirror. Mirrors reflect up to 95 percent of the light that hits them, while ordinary glass reflects only eight percent. How is this possible?

Fairground mirrors are made to be curved (with concave and convex surfaces) to make people's faces and bodies look odd.

Working layers

When light hits a mirror, it bounces straight back in the direction it came from. You see an exact reflection in modern mirrors because they're made from glass that has several layers of metal and chemicals applied to the back. These give the mirror strength and stability and make sure it gives a clear reflection.

Reflective silver layer (atoms shown magnified)

Backing

Glass

Convex mirror

Silver service

One of the best materials for creating reflections is silver. It forms a flat, smooth surface similar to the face of a large crystal. Polished silver reflects light well and gives a sharp image. On its own, though, silver tarnishes in air, so to make mirrors, it's applied directly to glass, then other layers are added on the back for protection.

Magnified silver crystals

Concave

Convex

Taking a curve

Curved mirrors give weird reflections and make you look very fat or thin. Concave mirrors dip in—they make things look larger but you see a smaller area reflected. Convex mirrors bulge out—they make things look smaller, but you see more.

When was the silvered-glass mirror invented?

Ancient images

In the Middle Ages, mirrors were made from polished stone, silver, bronze, or copper. These were very dark, and the metals became dull and discolored, so they produced spotty images.

weird or what?
We all go through life without ever really seeing our own faces—we can only ever see a reflection of it.

The world of mirrors

Even when you can't see them, there are mirrors everywhere!

Light-enhancing mirrors hung in wealthy homes for thousands of years. Before electricity was invented, they reflected candlelight.

Magnifying mirrors have a small, concave surface. They're designed to help in applying makeup or examining facial skin.

Dental mirrors help the dentist see all the hidden places inside your mouth. They're small and have handles.

Rearview mirrors are often convex to show a larger area. They're used on bicycles, cars, and trucks so drivers can see things behind the car.

Car headlights and flashlights both have mirrors behind their bulbs to make their beams stronger and straighter.

Sunglasses sometimes have one-way mirror lenses. These are slightly see-through, so you can see the world, but other people just see mirrors.

Reflector telescopes have mirrors set inside them to help gather and focus light.

Mirror

Hide and seek

Periscopes use mirrors to bend light so people can see around corners. A simple periscope is a tube with angled mirrors set parallel to each other at each end.

Light

Mirror

Spectators use mini periscopes to watch a golf tournament.

Military uses

Complex periscopes in submarines allow the crew to see the ocean's surface when they're underneath it. Periscopes are also used in tanks and gun turrets.

Lenses

Lenses are used to bend light to form an image. You have a lens in each eye, while telescopes and microscopes use lenses to help us see things that are either too far away or too small to be visible.

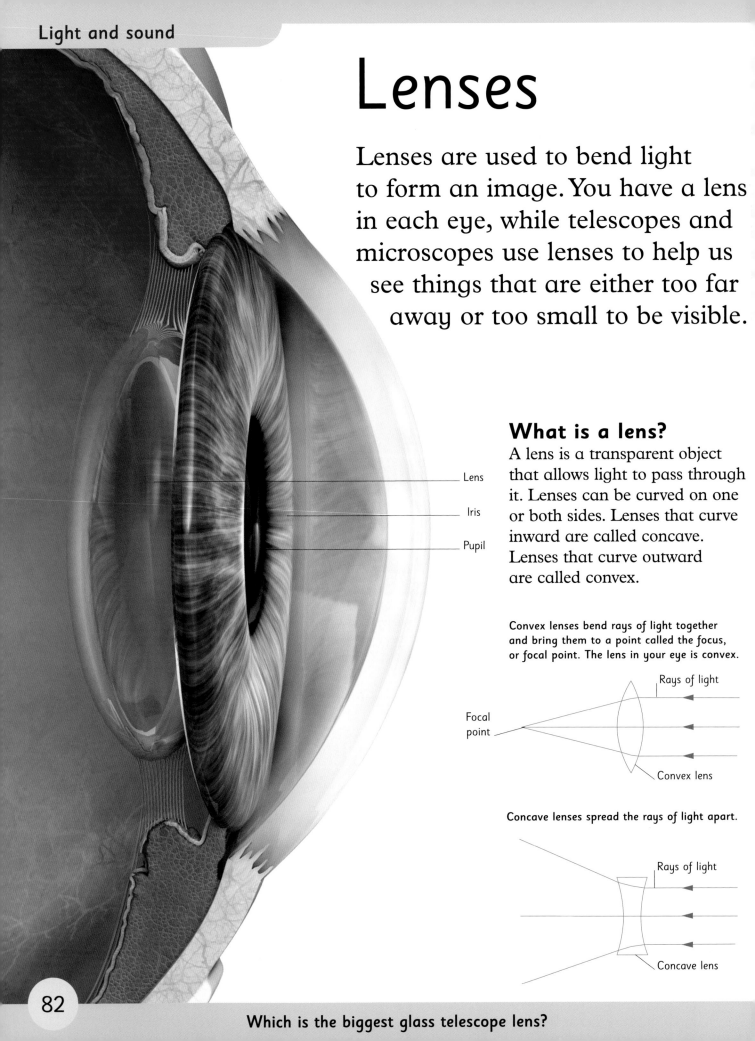

Lens

Iris

Pupil

What is a lens?

A lens is a transparent object that allows light to pass through it. Lenses can be curved on one or both sides. Lenses that curve inward are called concave. Lenses that curve outward are called convex.

Convex lenses bend rays of light together and bring them to a point called the focus, or focal point. The lens in your eye is convex.

Rays of light

Focal point

Convex lens

Concave lenses spread the rays of light apart.

Rays of light

Concave lens

Which is the biggest glass telescope lens?

How do your eyes work?

When you look at an object, the light from it travels in straight lines to the lens of your eye. The lens focuses the light upside down onto the retina at the back of your eye. Cells in the retina turn the image into an electrical message—a set of nerve signals. This travels to your brain, which interprets these signals and perceives the object the right way up.

hands on

Make a simple water lens. Put a piece of clear plastic over a magazine page and drip water onto it. Now look at the letters through the "lens." Do they look bigger?

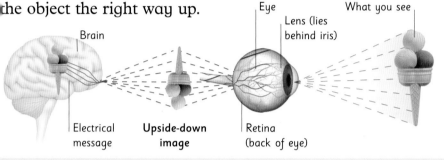

Brain

Eye

Lens (lies behind iris)

What you see

Electrical message

Upside-down image

Retina (back of eye)

That's better!

If someone is nearsighted, distant objects look blurred. This is because the lens focuses light in front of the retina instead of on it. If farsighted, nearby objects are blurred because light focuses behind the retina. Glasses or contact lenses help the eye focus light in the right place.

Nearsightedness

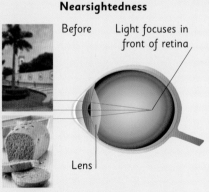

Before

Light focuses in front of retina

Lens

After

Nearsighted people can focus on things that are close but not those at a distance. Concave lenses lengthen the light's path through the eye.

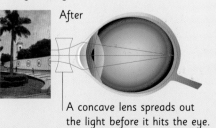

A concave lens spreads out the light before it hits the eye.

Farsightedness

Before

Light focuses behind the retina

After

Farsighted people can focus on things that are at a distance but not on close objects. Convex lenses help shorten the light's path.

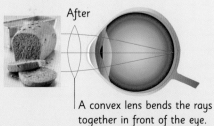

A convex lens bends the rays together in front of the eye.

Looking for lenses

You'll find lenses in all sorts of objects.

 Magnifying glasses are simple convex lenses that make things look bigger.

 Telescopes contain lenses that allow us to see things that are very far away.

 Microscopes make things that are too small for our eyes to see look bigger.

 Video projectors magnify images and direct them to a screen.

 Some cameras have a number of lenses to produce different effects.

Pupil shrinks in bright light

Bright light

Iris

Muscles around iris contract

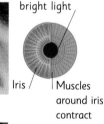

Pupil expands in dim light

Dim light

Muscles around iris relax

Instant reaction

There are muscles in the eye that help the lens change shape so you can change focus quickly to look at things that are near or far away. Other muscles around the iris control how much light enters the eye. Your pupils get bigger to allow more light in and help you see in dim conditions.

83

How light works

For thousands of years, the only lighting available was fire, oil lamps, candles—and later, gas lamps. Modern-day electric lights are more convenient and safe.

X-ray of an energy-efficient bulb

Wires inside the fitting carry electricity to electrodes.

Transformer boosts the voltage of the electricity supply.

Tungsten electrodes release electrons from electric current.

Gas molecules inside the glass tube give off invisible ultraviolet light.

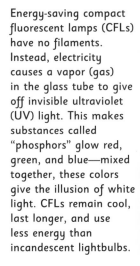

Basic bulbs

Old-style incandescent lightbulbs contain a small coil, or filament, made from tungsten—a strong metal that can get incredibly hot without melting. When an electric current passes though the tungsten coil, it gets so hot that it glows, and it's this glow that provides us with light.

Energy-saving compact fluorescent lamps (CFLs) have no filaments. Instead, electricity causes a vapor (gas) in the glass tube to give off invisible ultraviolet (UV) light. This makes substances called "phosphors" glow red, green, and blue—mixed together, these colors give the illusion of white light. CFLs remain cool, last longer, and use less energy than incandescent lightbulbs.

LEDs can be used for signs and outdoor display screens. They give off a very bright light and come in lots of different colors.

LED bulb

Lead connecting to electricity supply

Small and bright

Tiny pieces of semiconductor material called light-emitting diodes (LEDs) are used to produce light in all kinds of devices—and increasingly in lamps, too. They produce light by passing electricity through a special material that gives off light of one particular color.

How many bulbs are used to light the Empire State Building in New York City?

Mixing colors

White light is a mixture of the countless colors of the spectrum. But our eyes work in a way that means that the mix of just red, green, and blue light looks white. If you direct a ray of light through a prism, it splits into different colors. A mixture of two colors produces either magenta pink, yellow, or cyan blue.

The area where red, green, and blue mix together appears white.

Lasers

Lasers are devices that emit thin, powerful light beams. The light waves in a laser are all the same wavelength and line up exactly. This makes laser beams so intense they can cut through metal. Lasers are used in surgery, CD players, surveying, and industries.

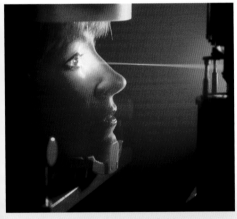

Lasers are used to treat eye problems such as nearsightedness.

Laser surgery

Lasers are used for many types of surgery. The light's energy is used to burn through tissue without cutting it with a scalpel. Lasers are also used to shatter kidney stones and shape cavities for fillings in dentistry.

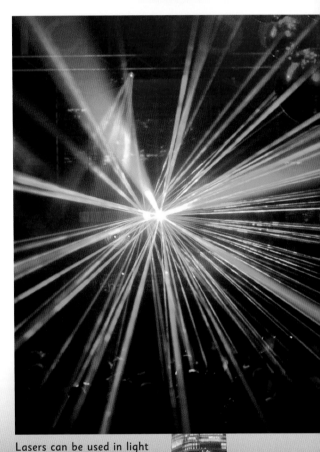

Lasers can be used in light shows and displays.

The Empire State Building uses 3,194,547 bulbs.

Fireworks

Fireworks are packets of chemicals that explode into bursts of color and noise when lit. A fuse ensures the explosion is delayed.

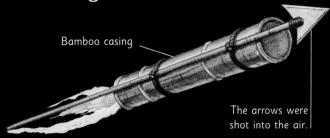

Bamboo casing

The arrows were shot into the air.

First fireworks

It's thought that the first fireworks were used in China more than 2,000 years ago. They were made from bamboo and used in religious ceremonies and to celebrate the New Year. Fire-arrows, like the one shown above, were rocketlike weapons that developed from fireworks.

High tech displays

Firework displays are often run by computers. The computer sends an electric spark down a wire to light each fuse. It makes fireworks launch in the right order and explode at their highest points in the sky.

3, 2, 1, liftoff!

Light the fuse and stand far back! The flame travels up into the firework where it quickly sets fire to gunpowder inside.

6. Explosion!
The chemicals inside the firework explode, releasing their energy as light, heat, and sound. Bang!

5. Stars
The gunpowder is mixed with stars—chemical mixtures that produce flashes of color.

4. Gunpowder
Explosive gunpowder is stored in a chamber inside the firework.

3. Propellant
Inside the cardboard case, gunpowder burns quickly to shoot the rocket skyward.

2. Fuse
Fuse paper contains chemicals that burn steadily to allow a person time to stand back after lighting.

1. Launch tube
In big displays, fireworks are put inside metal tubes to set them at the correct angles. These stay on the ground.

What is the firework called the Catherine Wheel named after?

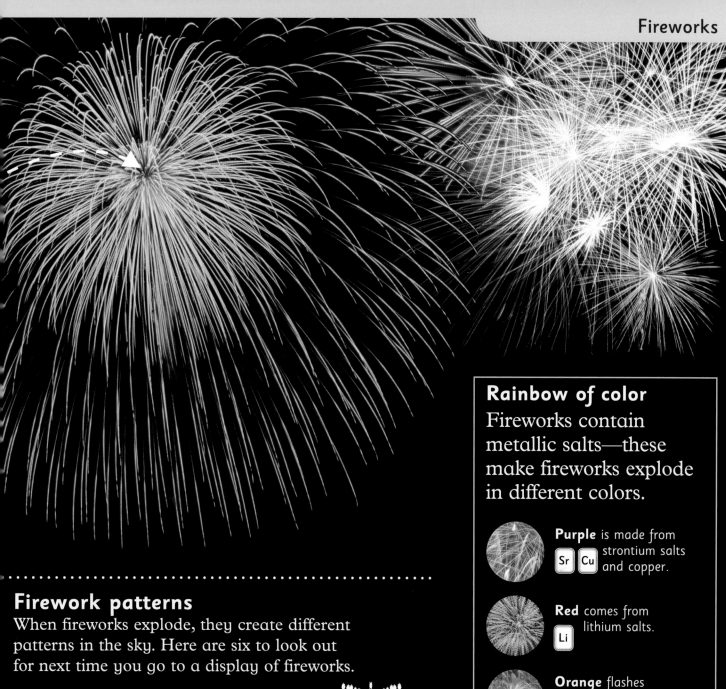

Rainbow of color

Fireworks contain metallic salts—these make fireworks explode in different colors.

Purple is made from strontium salts and copper. Sr Cu

Red comes from lithium salts. Li

Orange flashes are created by calcium salts. Ca

Yellow color comes from sodium compounds. Na

Green lights are made using barium compounds. Ba

Blue flashes come from copper compounds. Cu

Firework patterns

When fireworks explode, they create different patterns in the sky. Here are six to look out for next time you go to a display of fireworks.

Ring shell—a bright, expanding ring of stars.

Palm trees—stars move up as a "trunk," then spread out as "branches."

Chrysanthemum—a pattern that leaves long trails of stars.

Serpentine—many stars that zigzag outward as they fall.

Fish—a swarm of stars moving randomly across the sky.

Willow—star trails fall nearly all the way to the ground.

87

Measuring sound

All the sounds we hear are made up of waves that travel through the air to our ears. We can record the waves to see their shapes. Different sounds make waves of different shapes.

What is sound?

Sound is made up of waves of vibrations moving through the air. Any object that vibrates (moves quickly back and forth) can make a sound, just like this drum.

Sound waves

Sound waves spread out in all directions from where they are made. As a wave moves through the air, the air molecules are squeezed together and then stretched apart.

Hitting the drum skin with drum sticks makes it vibrate.

Sound waves

The skin of a drum is stretched very tight.

When you hit a drum, its skin vibrates up and down. Sometimes you can even see the skin moving. As the skin vibrates, it pushes and pulls on the air around it, making the air vibrate, too.

hands on
Hold one end of a rubber band on the edge of a table. Stretch out the other end and then pluck the rubber band. Can you see vibrations and hear the sound they make?

Can you hear sound in outer space?

We can pick up sound with a microphone. Inside it is a thin metal plate that vibrates when a sound wave hits it. The microphone turns the pattern of the vibrations into an electrical signal.

Microphone

Flatter sound waves have a small amplitude. They sound quiet.

Crest (top of wave)

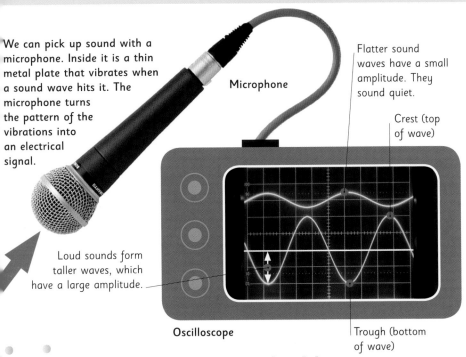

Loud sounds form taller waves, which have a large amplitude.

Oscilloscope

Trough (bottom of wave)

What sound looks like

Sound waves can be shown on a machine called an oscilloscope. The height of a wave is called its amplitude. The crests show where air is squeezed and the troughs show where air is stretched.

Slower than light

Sound waves travel slower than light. You can tell this during a thunderstorm. First you see the lightning, then you hear the thunder, perhaps several seconds later. Yet, they happen at the same time.

A loud, explosive storm

Decibel levels

The loudness of any sound is measured from a standard distance of 3 ft (1m) and in units called decibels (dB).

Leaves rustling
30 dB

Speaking
60 dB

Vacuum cleaner
70 dB

Busy traffic
80 dB

Baby crying
85 dB

!
85 dB

Pneumatic drill
125 dB

Listening to sounds of 85 dB and above for a long time can damage your ears.

Jet engine
140 dB

Frequency and pitch

Frequency is the number of crests on a sound wave that pass by each second. High-frequency sounds, such as bird song, sound high-pitched. Sounds with low frequency, like thunder, are low-pitched.

Sonic boom

Sound waves travel through air at about 745 mph

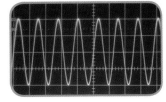

High-frequency sound waves

(1,200 kph). When a plane travels faster than the speed of sound, it creates sonic boom—a "shock wave" that makes a very loud noise.

No. There's no sound because there's no air for sound waves to travel through.

How ears hear

Sound travels in waves. When these waves reach your ears, they're carried to your brain, which tells you what sound you're hearing— your friend's voice, for example, or the pop of a bursting balloon.

Outer ear

Earwax is produced in the ear canal.

The stapes bone in your middle ear is the smallest bone in your body.

Ear, ear, ear

Your ears have three parts—the outer ear is the part you see. Your eardrum, which separates the outer ear from the middle ear, picks up sound vibration and passes it onto the three tiny bones of the middle ear. The inner ear contains bone, liquid, and tiny hairs, which turn the vibrations into signals to the brain.

Sound waves

This tunnel in the outer ear is called the ear canal.

The part of your ears that's on the outside of your head helps "catch" sound waves. The strange folds in your ears help you figure out when sounds are behind or above you.

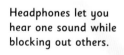

Headphones let you hear one sound while blocking out others.

weird or what?

People often suffer hearing loss (deafness) when they get old. But if you listen to very loud music all the time, or sit too near the speakers at rock concerts, your hearing could be damaged forever.

Sounds reach one ear before the other, which helps your brain figure out where they are.

Better than one

Ears are really very smart—they not only identify sounds, but can also tell how far away they are, and from which direction they're coming.

90

Are there any sounds we can't hear?

All change

When a sound enters your ears, it vibrates inside. The vibration is picked up by liquid in the inner ear, which vibrates slightly, causing tiny hairs to move. Cells at the base of these hairs transform the vibration into electrical impulses that travel along nerve pathways to your brain.

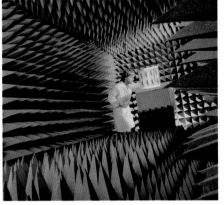

In an echo-free chamber, all the surfaces are lined with fiberglass wedges that absorb sound.

Hello
Hello

Echoes happen when sound waves bounce off one surface onto another and another and another, getting weaker every time they hit your ears.

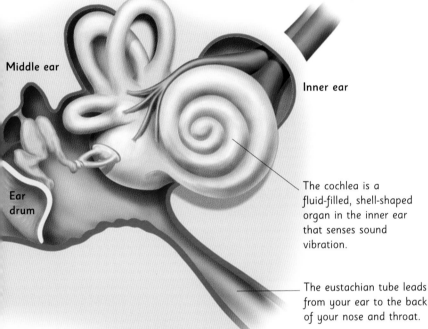

Middle ear

Inner ear

Ear drum

The cochlea is a fluid-filled, shell-shaped organ in the inner ear that senses sound vibration.

The eustachian tube leads from your ear to the back of your nose and throat.

Repeating sound

Sometimes you hear a sound once, then over and over again, getting fainter every time. This is called an echo. You can hear echoes in small spaces with hard walls, such as wells, or where there are lots of hard surfaces all around—in a canyon, cave, or mountain range.

Helping ear

Hearing can get damaged or worn out. If any sound gets through, a hearing aid will make it louder. Cochlear implants do more than this—they stimulate nerves in the cochlea, so they can help those who are totally deaf.

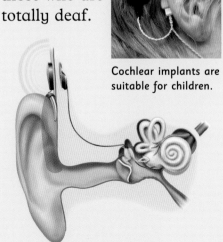

Cochlear implants are suitable for children.

Whispering walls

Sometimes, a hard, curved surface causes sound to behave in strange ways. Visitors to the dam at the Barossa Reservoir in South Australia can whisper at one end, and someone at the other end—over 460 ft (140 m) away—can hear them clearly. This is because the curve causes the sound waves to bounce in a series of jumps that run all along the length of the wall.

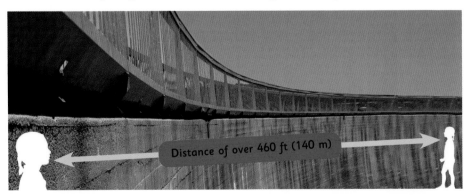

Distance of over 460 ft (140 m)

Yes—some sounds have such high frequency we can't hear them, but dogs, snakes, and bats can.

Electric guitar

When you pluck the strings of a traditional (acoustic) guitar, the sound is magnified in the guitar's hollow body. An electric guitar's body is solid, but it still makes a very loud noise!

Plectrum

You can pluck the strings with your fingers or a plectrum.

Frets show the musician where to place her fingers to change the note.

Six or twelve metal **strings** are each tuned to a different note.

1 Pluck the strings

Play an electric guitar without a pickup. The strings vibrate, but the sound they make is as quiet as a whisper.

The **bridge** has a **saddle** that lifts the strings clear of the pickup so they can vibrate easily.

The **neck** carries the fingerboard and supports the strings.

The **solid body** is made from a single piece of wood.

An amplifier boosts the electrical signals to make the sound loud.

Pickups detect the vibrations of the strings.

2 What picks up the sound?

A pickup has magnets with wire wrapped around them. A magnet has a magnetic field around it. When strings vibrate, they change the pattern of the magnetic field, creating electricity, which is transferred through the coil to the amplifier.

What is an amp?

3 Amplified

The electrical signal travels from the pickup along a wire to the amplifier. The amplifier strengthens the signal. A built-in loudspeaker then blasts out the electric guitar sound.

MAGNETIC FIELD

Guitar string

Magnet in pickup

Close-up view of a pickup

Signals travel to amplifier

Coil of wire

MAGNETIC FIELD

Machine heads are like screws and can be twisted to tighten or loosen the strings for tuning.

Volume and tone control knobs

Pickups convert vibrations from the strings into electrical signals.

The electrical current, or signal, from the pickup travels through wires to the controls, then onward to the amplifier.

Coil of wire in pickup

weird or what?

The electric guitar was first championed by jazz musicians. They loved the way this loud instrument let them be heard above the noise of a brass band.

Different electric guitars

Guitars come in all kinds of shapes and sizes. The shape of an electric guitar does not affect its sound.

Semi-acoustic guitars are a mix of electric and acoustic, with hollow bodies.

Bass guitars only have four strings and play the lower notes in a piece of music.

Double-headed guitars let musicians switch sounds without switching guitars.

Custom guitars are whatever shape or size a musician prefers.

93

Chips and codes

Digital technology relies on the microchip, which contains electrical circuits, and on binary codes, which instruct the hardware. Both work together to run electronic devices.

What's inside?
A silicon chip contains millions of transistors (things that control the flow of an electric current) and other tiny electronic parts that are all connected to one another.

Silicon chips
The world of electronics changed forever when, in 1961, inventor Robert Noyce created the silicon computer chip—a circuit cut into a piece of silicon. Silicon was chosen because it's a good semiconductor—it can keep the flow of electricity going or make it stop.

A silicon chip can be very small—less than $1/10$ sq in (1 sq cm) and about $1/100$ in (0.5 mm) thick.

Sand covers over half the Earth's surface.

Lump of silicon

Ever heard of silicon?
Silicon and oxygen make up sand. Once pure silicon is separated from sand, it can be used to make microchips.

How many transistors can fit on a single silicon chip?

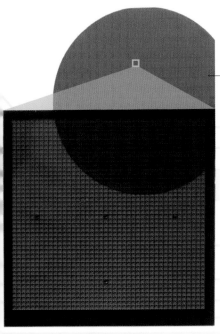

Silicon wafer

How is a silicon chip made?

Electronic circuit patterns are photographed onto disks of silicon, called wafers. Chemicals are used to etch the patterns into the silicon in several layers. The wiring that connects the circuit is made in the same way.

Pattern to be etched on chip

Individual chips

Wafers are tested to make sure they work. After being checked, they are cut into individual chips, which are placed in protective cases.

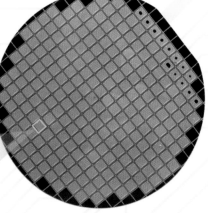

Individual chip from wafer

Hundreds of chips can be made on a single wafer.

Finished chip in package

Codes

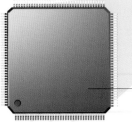

Transistors on a microchip act like switches that can either be off (interpreted as "zero") or on (interpreted as "one") when electricity passes through them. The one and zero form basic binary codes that tell the device what to do.

Picture detective

Look through the Digital world pages and see if you can identify the picture clues below.

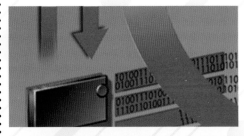

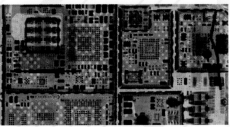

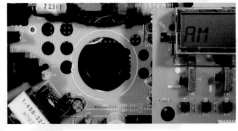

Turn and learn

Binary code:
pp. 98–99

The Internet:
pp. 110–111

95

Inside a computer

We use computers to do all kinds of things—play games, watch videos, and surf the Internet. All these things are controlled by a microprocessor that acts like a tiny electronic brain.

The microprocessor, or central processing unit (CPU), is the single most important chip in a computer. This electronic circuit is what makes all the programs run. It is placed inside the computer.

A computer stores programs and files on a hard disk or a solid state drive. These typically store hundreds of gigabytes of data.

Laptop computer

All the components of a personal computer can be built into a convenient folding package the size of a book. Laptops use wireless technology to interact with printers, scanners, and other devices by radio waves.

Instead of a mouse, a trackpad is used to control the cursor on screen. By dragging a finger over the trackpad and clicking buttons, it is easy to scroll vertically and horizontally, or open and close windows.

How a motherboard works

The motherboard is the main circuit board in a computer. It connects all the main parts and passes on instructions.

2 I/O controller makes the central processing unit (CPU) pause.

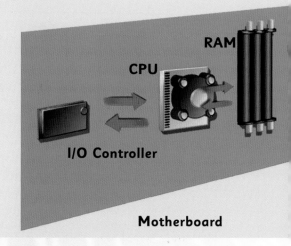

RAM

CPU

I/O Controller

Motherboard

1 Keyboard communicates with motherboard via input/output (I/O) controller.

What is a netbook?

Computer screens display any color, by combining light from millions of tiny red, green, and blue dots.

Ports provide connections to external devices. An MP3 player, digital camera, Internet dongle, or external hard drive can be plugged into various ports. You can also transfer your photos and videos using a memory card slot.

Computer talk
Many internal and external parts come together to make a computer work.

Memory holds data that the CPU needs to read and write quickly.

Secondary storage—hard disks and solid state drives—store programs and files.

1MB All data on a computer is held in units called **bytes**.

Cables connect the laptop to input devices, printers, and the Internet.

Input devices include computer mouses, joysticks, and drawing tablets.

weird or what?

Engineers have designed portable computers that can be worn on the body and controlled using eyeblinks.

3 CPU stops what it is doing and accesses memory (RAM) to run the keyboard driver built into the program.

4 Keyboard driver finds out what key was pressed and what character this represents.

Graphics processing unit

5 CPU tells the graphics processing unit (GPU) to put that character on the screen.

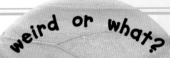

6 Monitor displays characters on screen

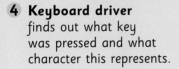

Binary code

The binary code is made up of two digits: 1 and 0. Images, text, and sounds can all be converted into this code so a computer can understand them.

A binary system—having only two digits or options—is also used by Morse code (dots and dashes) and Braille (raised and flat dots).

Bit

A **bit** is a binary digit, and can be either a 0 or a 1. Each bit can hold the answer to one simple question, using 0 for "No" and 1 for "Yes."

Byte

A **byte** is made up of 8 bits, and is the measurement unit used to describe the storage capacity and transfer rate of digital systems.

1 **kilobyte** is 1,000 bytes
1 **megabyte** is 1,000 kilobytes
1 **gigabyte** is 1,000 megabytes
1 **terabyte** is 1,000 gigabytes
1 **petabyte** is 1,000 terabytes
1 **exabyte** is 1,000 petabytes

Binary numbering

Computers use binary numbers because they are easier to handle. In binary, the digits (read from the right) are worth 1, 2, 4, 8, and so on—not units, tens, and hundreds. In ordinary numbers, "1001" is one unit, no tens, no hundreds, and one thousand. But in binary, "1001" is one 1, no 2, no 4, and one 8, which equals 9.

How many ones and zeros can a fiber-optic cable carry per second?

Sending numbers

Fiber-optic cables are used to transport binary numbers from one computer to another. An electric current carries the numbers as a stream of digital data. A laser turns the current into pulses of light that are sent through the fiber-optic cable.

The first signal is sent down the middle.

A cable used for telecommunications has 100 or more optical cables inside.

A central steel cable protects the fibers.

A second signal travels in a zigzag line.

A polymer outer sheath keeps the fiber safe from damage.

The center is made from glass or plastic.

A third signal travels by reflection but doesn't get in the way of other signals.

Light is reflected back into the core by glass or plastic cladding.

Origins of binary

Inspired by ancient Indian and Chinese ideas, the German mathematician Gottfried Leibniz first developed the early form of the binary number system in the 17th century.

ASCII Code: character to binary code

0	0011 0000	F	0100 0110	U	0101 0101
1	0011 0001	G	0100 0111	V	0101 0110
2	0011 0010	H	0100 1000	W	0101 0111
3	0011 0011	I	0100 1001	X	0101 1000
4	0011 0100	J	0100 1010	Y	0101 1001
5	0011 0101	K	0100 1011	Z	0101 1010
6	0011 0110	L	0100 1100		
7	0011 0111	M	0100 1101		
8	0011 1000	N	0100 1110		
9	0011 1001	O	0100 1111		
A	0100 0001	P	0101 0000		
B	0100 0010	Q	0101 0001		
C	0100 0011	R	0101 0010		
D	0100 0100	S	0101 0011		
E	0100 0101	T	0101 0100		

For lower case letters "a" to "o" start with 0110, while for "p" to "z" start with 0111. The next four digits are the same as for upper case, so a = 0110 0001.

hands on

Using the code below, you can write out your name in binary code. Use uppercase letters for the beginning letter of your first and last name, and lowercase for the remaining letters.

Sharing data

When you send an email or a message on your mobile phone, how does it know where to go? In fact, it is passed around a huge series of computers that are connected to one another by wires or radio.

Without a wire

Many devices can connect to a network wirelessly, using radio waves. Wi-Fi provides the most common way to connect, but Bluetooth is also popular. It allows devices to connect together one-to-one, forming a "personal area network."

Laptop computers and smartphones connect wirelessly to the router. They allow people to communicate from anywhere in the house.

Smart devices

Some people have digital devices at home that have computers inside them. These "smart" devices are connected to the router and can gather information or stream content from the Internet.

Smart speakers can be controlled by voice commands.

Bluetooth headphones allow wearers to listen to music on their phone without a wire connecting them. That's useful if you are carrying your phone in your pocket.

How does it work?

Just like TVs and FM radios, a wireless system uses radio waves. It chops up data into manageable pieces and transmits that data in separate chunks as radio waves. The receiving device, such as a phone or computer, picks up the radio signals and puts the data back together.

How far can Bluetooth connect wireless devices?

What are computer networks?

Towns and cities are joined together by a network of roads. Computers and other devices are also linked together by networks. The scale of a network can be as small as a home computer and printer or as big as hundreds of computers used in an office.

Antenna

Most devices connect to a router using Wi-Fi, a wireless technology that uses radio waves to send and receive data. Some devices connect by cables plugged into the back of the router instead.

Home network router

At the heart of a computer network is a device called a router. It links other devices on the network to one another, and to the Internet. It allows devices in the home to communicate with other devices across the world.

Networks
There are many different types of network used to link computers.

PAN Personal Area Networks are used for single-user devices.

LAN Local Area Networks can join small groups of computers, like those in an office.

CAN Campus Area Networks link university campus LANs into one network.

MAN Metropolitan Area Networks connect all the networks in a city.

WAN Wide Area Networks cover large areas across national or international boundaries.

GAN Global Area Networks connect many WANs over a huge geographical area.

Smart televisions can display ordinary television broadcasts but are also able to stream films from a variety of online providers.

What is a server?

Servers are computers that hold information for other connected devices to access. Servers are particularly important on the Internet. The two most important kinds are web servers, which store web pages and the images they contain, and mail servers, which store emails that users can download when they log in.

Cell phones

Spread out across the world is a network of tall metal towers, called base stations. When you call someone from your cell, the call travels to the nearest base station, which sends it on an incredibly fast journey to the receiver's phone. It takes only a few seconds to make the connection.

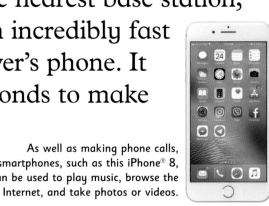

As well as making phone calls, smartphones, such as this iPhone® 8, can be used to play music, browse the Internet, and take photos or videos.

Early cell phones weighed about 28 oz (800 g).

Early phones
In the 1980s, phones were as big as bricks—far larger than phones today.

Cell networks
Cell phones work within a network of cells. Each cell is covered by a base station. You can only make a call if you are within a particular range of a base station.

Base station
In the countryside, base stations cover larger areas than in cities. This is because there are fewer people living in rural areas, so fewer people use the network.

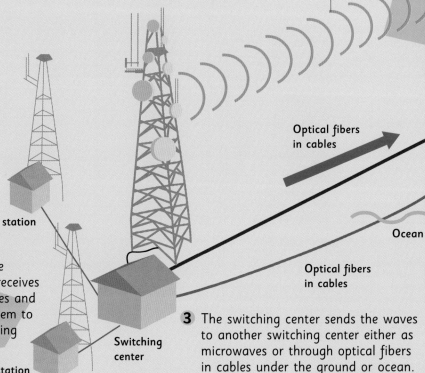

Microwave link

Optical fibers in cables

Ocean

Optical fibers in cables

Base station

Base station

Switching center

Cell phone

1 A cell encodes sound into radio waves. It sends out these waves to the nearest base station.

2 The base station receives the waves and sends them to a switching center.

3 The switching center sends the waves to another switching center either as microwaves or through optical fibers in cables under the ground or ocean.

What does SIM stand for?

What do they do?

Cell phones have lots of good features and some bad ones.

 Make calls, send texts, make video clips, and take photos.

 Play music, download video clips, and watch television programs.

 Find directions, get train times, and download listings of what's going on.

 Cells create waste because they take hundreds of years to break down.

weird or what?

Every minute, all over the world, 1,000 people buy a cell phone for the first time. There are more than three billion cell phones in the world and more are made each day.

What's inside?

Inside every cell there is an antenna to send and receive calls and messages, an electric circuit board to run the phone, a loudspeaker, a microphone, and a battery to provide power.

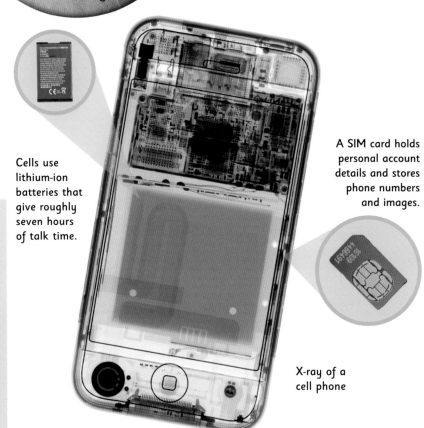

Cells use lithium-ion batteries that give roughly seven hours of talk time.

A SIM card holds personal account details and stores phone numbers and images.

X-ray of a cell phone

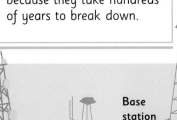

Switching center

Base station

Base station

Cell phone

4 The switching center sends the waves to another base station.

5 This base station sends the waves to another phone.

Text messages travel over the same network as digitized sounds. Billions of text messages are sent every day.

Watch phones

Smartwatches, also called watch phones, can be worn on your wrist and used to perform certain cell phone functions, such as make and receive calls, take photos or videos, and show maps to help you find your way.

A Samsung Gear 3 smartwatch

Subscriber identity module.

Digital photography

Digital cameras allow you to capture a moment in time, such as blowing out your birthday candles. They are also used in space exploration and medical science.

hands on

Ask an adult if you can you use a digital camera to take a photo or record a video of something in your home.

Lens   Shutter   Flash

When it is too dark to take a photo, an built-in flash briefly lights up the scene.

Take a pic!
Digital cameras vary in size, from a small camera on a cell phone to a large professional studio camera. Many people own a compact camera or a DSLR (digital single lens reflex) camera like this one.

From light to a digital file
So how does a camera actually take a photo? It's a simple process that needs the following in order to work: light, a shutter, a lens, a sensor, and a memory card.

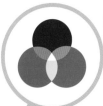

Light is made up of three primary colors: red, green, and blue. By combining these colors of light, you can create any other color. All three combined make white light.

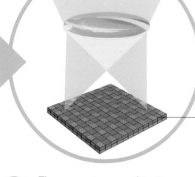

The sensor is a grid of millions of pixels.

1 Light is reflected off a scene. The camera's shutter opens so this light can pass through the lens to a sensor inside the camera.

2 The sensor is covered in tiny squares, called pixels. Each pixel measures the amount of red, green, or blue light that hit it. Each pixel is recorded using binary code (see pp. 98–99).

3 This binary coded information travels to the camera's memory system, where it is stored on the memory card. It can be viewed, stored, and edited on a computer.

How many pixels are in a megapixel?

View, focus, take!

Some digital cameras have a viewfinder to allow photographers to see what they want to photograph. Other cameras just have a screen on the back of the camera for composing a shot.

Pixels

Seeing an image

Images shown on a digital camera screen are made up of thousands of tiny pixels. When you look at all the pixels together, they make a complete image.

Viewfinder

Canon

The dial allows the user to choose different settings, such as the flash or close-up shots.

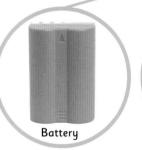

Battery

Most digital cameras use rechargeable batteries.

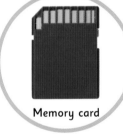

Memory card

Images are stored on removable memory cards. You can download them onto your computer.

Saving memories

Old-fashioned film cameras store images directly onto plastic film, whereas digital cameras record photos on memory cards. The space in the memory card is measured in megabytes (MB) and gigabytes (GB), and it can vary from just 512 MB to a massive 128 GB! Memory cards are likely to increase in capacity in the future.

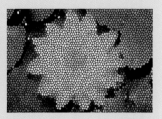

The most exciting thing about taking digital photos is viewing them! You can download images by inserting a memory card into a computer or through a cable attaching the camera to a computer.

Editing and playing with photos

Digital photos can be edited and changed in special computer programs. You can play with an image, make it black and white, or you can fix red-eye. Try out the examples below.

Convert to black and white

Play around with fun effects

Fix red-eye

Happy birthday!

Add text to an image

Who invented radio?

Guglielmo Marconi is credited with building the first radio system. In 1901, he transmitted radio signals across the Atlantic Ocean.

Radio and TV

It's hard to imagine life without radio or TV. We use them for information and entertainment. There are millions of programs, but how do they get to our radios and TVs?

How do radios work?

First called a wireless, the radio doesn't need wires to connect the transmitter and receiver.

 Speech and music are turned into electrical signals by a **microphone** in a radio studio.

 The **electrical signals** from the speech and music travel through wires to a **radio transmitter**.

 The **radio transmitter** sends out radio waves from the radio station.

 Traditional radio sets pick up the radio waves and turn them back into speech and music.

What's inside?

The main parts of a radio are an antenna, a circuit board with a tuner and amplifier, and a loudspeaker.

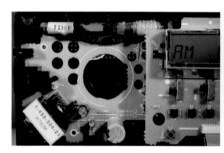

Digital radio

When you listen to a digital radio, there is little or no interference, for example, from hissing noises. Digital transmitters send out sound codes that are all mixed up together. The interference can't affect the codes much, and your radio will usually be able to understand them.

Digital transmission

Digital radios also use a transmitter, but the waves they use are different to those from a traditional radio.

Digital radios use codes made of lots of ones and zeros. They are transmitted over a large band of radio waves.

Antenna

The antenna is usually at the back of the radio It picks up the radio waves.

Inside the radio is a tuner and a computer chip that decodes the waves and converts them into sound.

What does LCD stand for?

A neon lamp sent light into holes in a spinning disk.

First TV

The scientific research for televisions began in the late 1800s. John Logie Baird's televisor was the first working TV. A rotating disk transformed light from a scene into lines forming a moving image.

TV inventor

In 1928, Baird demonstrated the first TV transmission across the Atlantic, and the first television program for the BBC in the UK.

Baird's televisor

Images on the televisor were grainy. The mechanical system was soon replaced with a better quality electronic system.

The light coming through the spinning disk lit up a scene and created a moving image. The red light from the neon lamp made the image appear red.

Transmission today

Television stations transmit programs through electrical waves.

 Television pictures are created by **cameras**, mostly in **studios**.

 Programs are sent out from the studio over **wires** as electrical waves or **microwaves.**

 Waves can be sent up to **satellites** in space and then sent back to Earth.

 Satellite dishes can pick up the microwaves and send them to TVs along a cable.

 A **TV** turns the waves into the pictures and sound that make up a TV program.

LCD TV

LCD (liquid crystal display) screens are used in TVs, calculators, and watches. LCD screens, and more recent OLED (organic light-emitting diode) screens, are made up of millions of tiny squares called pixels.

If you look very closely at an LCD TV screen, you can see the pixels.

Color squares

Pixels contain blue, red, and green color. The combination of different colors in the pixels form the images we see.

weird or what?
There are roughly 1.6 billion television sets in the world! That's one TV for every four people on the planet.

Liquid crystal display.

Bar codes

Bar codes make shopping faster and more convenient. A scanner reads an item's bar code, and it sends a code to a computer. The computer sends back information about that item, including its price.

From one code to another

The first bar code was invented in 1948 by US academic Bernard Silver. He was inspired by Morse code, which uses dots and dashes to encode letters. He extended Morse code marks into the long lines of a bar code.

S A L E

What is a bar code?

The black and white stripes of a bar code represent a string of numbers—a code that is unique to a single product. Various types of bar code exist. The type shown here is used throughout Europe.

Where's it from?

The first number in a bar code tells you the country where the product was made. Every country has its own number: Anything from 00 to 13 is in the US and Canada, and 50 means the UK.

Manufacturer's logo

Who makes it?

This is the code number of the manufacturer who made the product. All products made by that manufacturer will have the same four-digit code.

5 012345

What's your number?

Each number in a bar code is represented by two white stripes and two black stripes of different widths. The long, thin guide lines at the edges and center of the code tell the scanner to start reading.

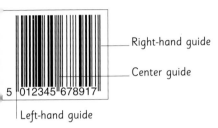

Right-hand guide

Center guide

5 012345 678917

Left-hand guide

Scanner

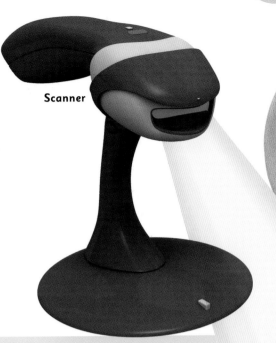

678917

Machine readable part
The scanners you normally find in the supermarket are known as "omni-directional" scanners. They emit laser light in a starburst pattern that can read the bar codes at any angle.

Human readable part
If the scanner is unable to read the bar code, the cashier can input the numbers.

What is it?
This is the code for the product itself. The code number for this item is 567891.

The check digit
This number is used by the scanner to check whether it has read the data correctly.

Scanning the goods

The scanner shines a narrow beam of light onto a bar code. A light sensor inside the scanner measures the reflected light. White lines reflect more light than black lines, which is how it tells the difference.

2-D bar codes

These new bar codes are scanned from top to bottom as well as left to right. Some of them can be read by cell phone cameras and webcams and take you straight to a website.

Some 2-D bar codes, like this Quick Response code, can store hundreds of times more information than ordinary bar codes.

On June 26, 1974, for a pack of chewing gum.

The Internet

People first found out about the Internet in the early 1990s, but it was used only by select groups (mostly military and educational) before then. Now about 3 billion people use it—over a quarter of the world's population.

WWW

The World Wide Web

Applications like the World Wide Web let you use the Internet for information, entertainment, and communication. People can even build their own websites for other people to use.

What is the Internet?

It's simply a network that links computers around the world. Try imagining it as a huge map (or spider's web), with all the strands linked by different pathways.

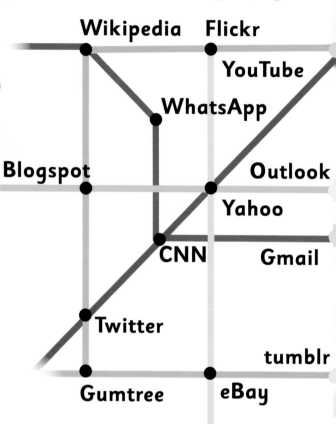

Wikipedia Flickr
YouTube
WhatsApp
Blogspot Outlook
Yahoo
CNN Gmail
Twitter
tumblr
Gumtree eBay

The Internet doesn't just link computers together; it also connects tablets, smartphones, and other smart devices.

INFORMATION

Find out about almost any subject that catches your interest by entering a few key words in a search engine.

GAMING

People all over the world play one another at MMOGs—massively multiplayer online games.

SHOPPING

Buy anything from a vacation to a pen without stepping outside. Every day, billions of things are sold online.

Make new friends and connect with people who have similar interests from around the world through social media channels.

SOCIAL MEDIA

What is Wi-Fi?

YOU ARE HERE

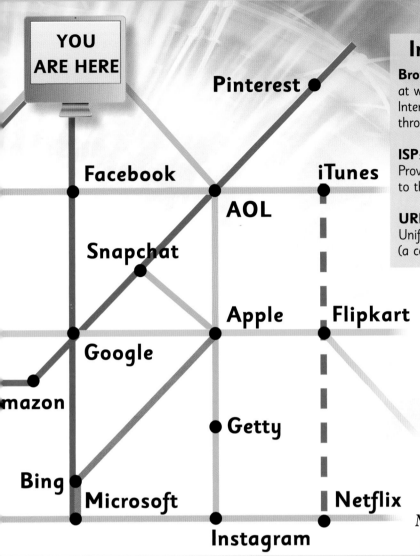

Pinterest

Facebook   iTunes

AOL

Snapchat

Apple   Flipkart

Google

mazon

Getty

Bing

Microsoft   Netflix

Instagram

Internet terminology

Browsing: Looking at web pages on the Internet and navigating through them.

ISP: Internet Service Providers link computers to the Internet.

URL: This stands for Uniform Resource Locator (a complete web address).

HTML: HyperText Markup Language is the language in which web pages are written.

Router: A device for routing Internet traffic.

Search engine: A site that holds a database of website addresses.

Web browsers

A web browser helps you find, retrieve, and look at web pages on the Internet. Most browsers can display not just words and pictures but also videos and sounds.

Press send

Splitting information into parcels or packets before it is sent to its destination is called packet switching. There's a portion of the original text, and the addresses of the computers it's traveling between.

Broken link

1 An image or email is broken into packets of data by the computer.

2 Binary digits in each packet represent pieces of the picture. Each packet is addressed to the destination computer.

3 The router sends the packet to its destination— different packets from the same image may take a different route.

4 The router tries to keep from using busy or broken links.

5 The destination computer sorts out all the packets and slots them back together again.

It's the technology that lets you access the Internet using radio waves instead of cables.

Search engines

The Internet contains a vast amount of information, and finding what you're after can be tricky unless you know how to look. Search engines are useful tools, since they do all the hard work for you.

How do search engines work?

Search engines use special robots called "spiders." These spiders search the Internet for new pages. They target websites that have a lot of traffic (people visiting them), then spread out to other web pages. The search engine lists the words on those pages and uses them to create an index.

1 Web spiders search the Internet for new web pages.

Apple	Highchair	Pianos
Backtrack	Iceland	Quail
Birch	Internal	Rested
Clearance	Jock	Sage
Dinner	Kilt	Sesame
Dinosaurs	Labrador	Souffle
Eating	Minimize	Traffic
Fruits	Orange	Uniform
Gluttonously	Organic	Unleaded
Hearing	Peony	Vest

2 Search engines list the words on each page the spiders find.

Bundle
Binary
Bicycle
Biceps
Banana

3 It then creates an index of all the words it finds.

4 A user types in a word.

bicycle

Good-quality bicycles
Children's bikes
Bicycle bargains
Bicycle

5 The search engine checks its index to find any relevant pages.

Bicycle bargains
Massive savings on bikes
www.bikesZ129.com

Children's bikes
New and used bicycles for children
www.NandUbikes3000.com

Good-quality bicycles
Buy brand new bicycles at cheap prices
www.cheapbikesforu99.com

6 It lists these pages for the user in a matter of seconds.

Where did the search engine Google get its name?

<u>Web</u>   <u>Images</u>   <u>Videos</u>   <u>Maps</u>   <u>News</u>   <u>Shopping</u>   <u>Mail</u>   <u>More</u>

Metadata

Websites often have key words (metadata) embedded in them. Businesses make sure their web pages contain these words in the title and subtitle of a web page. Web page designers can also highlight certain words to make sure search engines pick them up.

Complex searches

If you type in an exact quote, a question, or a few key words, a search engine will look for these words within web pages. These are literal searches, so they look for your exact wording. You need to be clear, or you won't find the information you want.

Searches

airplanes

⬇

British airplanes

⬇

British airplanes, 1940s

⬇

British airplanes, 1940s, used in WW2

Search terms

Working with the Internet involves lots of special words and expressions.

 http:// will appear in front of most Internet addresses you open.

 http stands for Hypertext Transfer Protocol, an information-transfer system.

 Bookmarks give you quick access to your favorite sites.

History facilities list recently accessed sites so you can go back to them.

Tags are key labels given to bookmarks or files so you can find them quickly.

If a website has lots of visitors, it's more likely to come first in a list.

Top of the list

Companies try to make sure that their web page comes at the top of all the search engine lists. They do this by putting key words on the site, or by paying search engines to put an ad for their company on the first page.

 weird or what? If a business doesn't want to be listed in searches, it can build a robot-exclusion protocol into its website so search spiders will ignore the page.

From the word "googol," which stands for the number 1 with 100 zeros after it.

Robots

Robots are computer-controlled machines that do tasks without the help of humans. Many robots are used for work in factories, but some do jobs at home.

The robot vacuum cleaner is powered by rechargeable batteries.

Home help

A robot vacuum cleaner moves around a room on its own, sucking up dust. To find its way, the robot sends out sound waves. These bounce off walls, tables, and chairs, so the robot knows where they are.

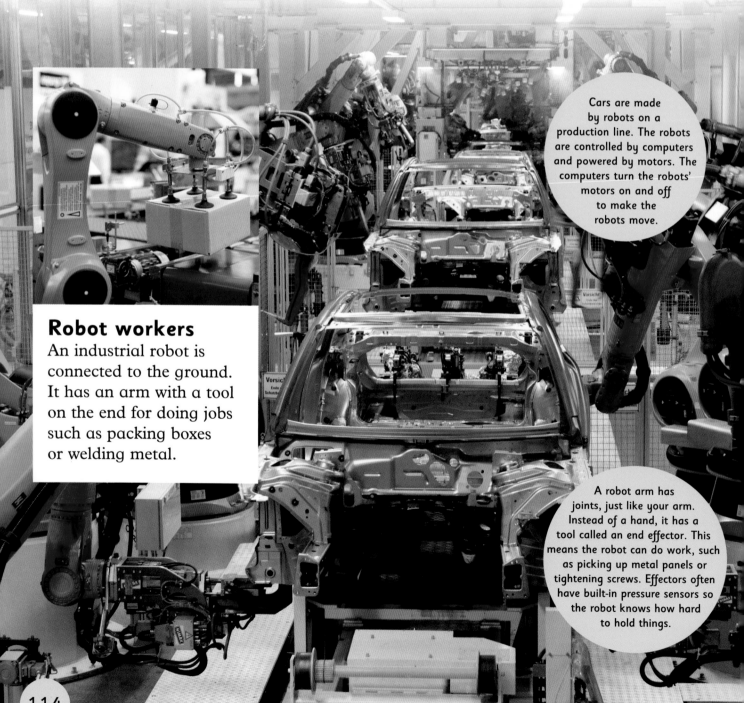

Cars are made by robots on a production line. The robots are controlled by computers and powered by motors. The computers turn the robots' motors on and off to make the robots move.

Robot workers

An industrial robot is connected to the ground. It has an arm with a tool on the end for doing jobs such as packing boxes or welding metal.

A robot arm has joints, just like your arm. Instead of a hand, it has a tool called an end effector. This means the robot can do work, such as picking up metal panels or tightening screws. Effectors often have built-in pressure sensors so the robot knows how hard to hold things.

How smart is the most intelligent robot?

Swarm robotics

The result of a new approach in robotics, swarm robots are designed to work together to perform a task. Some attach themselves to one another to make one machine. Others work like ants, completing tasks as a team.

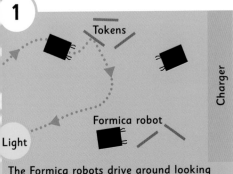

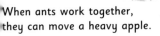
When ants work together, they can move a heavy apple.

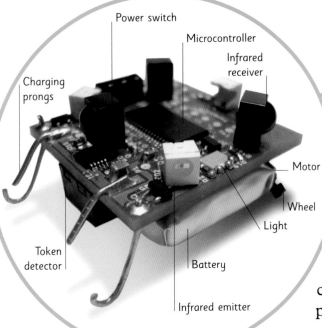

Power switch
Microcontroller
Infrared receiver
Charging prongs
Motor
Wheel
Light
Token detector
Battery
Infrared emitter

Formica— actual size

Formica robot

This micro robot uses infrared light to "talk" to other robots on its team. It can be programmed to perform different tasks, such as moving tokens toward a light.

1

Tokens
Formica robot
Light
Charger

The Formica robots drive around looking for tokens to push toward the light.

2

I saw a token 1 second ago

Light
Charger

When one robot meets another, it tells it how long ago it saw a token.

3

I saw a token 60 seconds ago

Abandon search. Return to charger

Light
Charger

The robots haven't seen a token for a while, so they return to the charger.

Humanoid robots

Today, engineers are trying to make humanoid robots—machines that look and behave like humans. Asimo is one of the world's most sophisticated humanoid robots. It can grasp objects, walk, run, climb stairs, and carry objects. It is also smart enough to recognize faces and gestures, and obey voice commands.

It took scientists more than two decades to create this advanced humanoid robot.

Bomb squad

Special military teams use remote-controlled robots to carry away bombs and other dangerous materials.

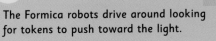

The future

Many of the advancements we see around us today—airplanes, cell phones, computers—were once thought to be impossible dreams. But scientists keep creating amazing things that can reshape the world and change our lives.

Computerized rooms

In smart homes, all electronic gadgets are connected to the owner's smartphone or tablet. So the owner can control a machine from anywhere.

Smart Home console

68°F /20°C

Living room
Statistics
Temperature
Setting

Smart TV — ON:1 OFF:0
Air Conditioner — ON:2 OFF:0
Light Setting — ON:0 OFF:3
Robot Cleaner — ON:1 OFF:0
Smoke Sensor — ON:2 OFF:0

This tablet computer uses a special program through which it connects with, and controls, electronic home appliances.

Xanadu Houses

The Xanadu Houses were designed and built in Florida. They were the pioneer for future houses, with high-tech energy-saving designs and automated rooms.

Computers will sense radio tags in clothes and objects to keep track of everything.

Roof and walls are made from a special plastic foam.

The plastic (polyurethane) foam traps heat and lowers energy bills. It is also quick and easy to build with.

When was the first Xanadu House built?

Inside a new world

Virtual reality is a computer-generated environment that gives people the feeling that they are actually part of an imaginary world. They have been used in movies, art, video games, and even military training exercises.

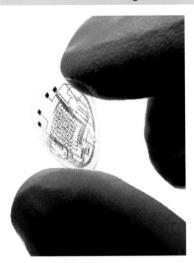

Bionic lenses

Researchers are developing contact lenses that will let the wearer see information, news, emails, and entertainment on a virtual screen. A basic version of the lenses has been made successfully. Scientists are now working to improve them.

Communication pole

The Xanadu House used computers to run it—from an auto-chef in the kitchen to a talking security computer.

weird or what? Today, smartfridges have touchscreen displays and are programmed to keep track of your food, alert you when supplies run low, and even order fresh food through the Internet.

The Xanadu House was a popular tourist attraction for over 10 years. After years of neglect, it was demolished in 2005.

The first experimental Xanadu House was built in Wisconsin in 1979.

Delivery drones

In the future, your online shopping might be delivered by drones (flying robots). Drones may also be used to deliver food and medicines to people stranded in earthquakes zones and other disaster areas.

Drones would find their own way to your home without the need for a pilot.

Maglev train

Maglev trains float, or "levitate," above the track, held in the air by magnetic forces. A maglev train uses much less fuel than a normal train, and can travel much faster.

There is no friction between a maglev train and the track, because they do not touch.

The hydrogen plane

Airplanes powered by electric motors, such as Element One (below), may become a common sight in the future, as they don't produce carbon emissions during flight. Hydrogen planes are powered by fuel cells which combine hydrogen with oxygen to release energy, and produce only water vapour as a waste product.

Self-driving cars

Cars that drive themselves have already undergone years of successful testing, and could soon be a common sight on the roads. Several cameras and other sensors monitor the road, nearby cars, and other obstacles, and feed information to a powerful computer that controls the car.

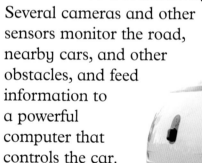

In a self-driving car, you could read or sleep while the car drives you to your destination.

When did the first zeppelin airship take to the skies?

Space vacations

Space is slowly becoming the ultimate luxury vacation destination. Vacationers pay large sums of money to be able to glimpse amazing views of the Earth from space, as well as experience zero gravity.

Virgin Galactic plans to offer people suborbital flights that give a taste of space.

The first space tourist was Dennis Tito, who paid millions of dollars to spend a week on board the International Space Station.

Return of the airship

Popular in the first half of the 20th century, airships may soon be a common sight in our skies. Powered by clean solar energy and helped by the wind, massive aircrafts, such as the Aeroscraft, won't need to refuel. Although they will be slower than airplanes, they will be able to lift heavy loads, making them perfect for transporting heavy cargo.

The major advantage of airships like the Aeroscraft is that it can take off or land vertically, eliminating the need for runways.

The first zeppelin airship flew in 1900.

Anytime soon?

The distant future offers many fantastic possibilities. Scientists could upgrade our brains, invent computer doctors who can diagnose at the touch of a button, and discover how to copy the way the sun works.

bonjour
hola
ciao
hello
hallo
hi
hälsningar
merhaba
halo
powitanie

Learn a new language in minutes by plugging it into your brain!

Brain upgrade

To upgrade a computer, new computer chips, memory boards, and software are plugged in and loaded. In the future, human brains could be upgraded in a similar way. The first plug-in modules could offer better memory, reactions, or language skills. Even entertainment could be tuned in, with 3-D shows and even smell-o-vision.

When the rain falls and temperature drops, smartclothes may become watertight and thick.

Clothes in the future may even change color to match other clothes and accessories.

Wearable technology

Innovators are trying to create technologically advanced fabrics. For example, smartclothes designed for athletes might have sensors that can monitor heart rate and respiration. Some companies are developing fabrics that are stronger than polyester, as well as being resistant to extreme heat and explosions. There may even be clothes with flexible displays and built-in GPS that can project videos, images, maps, and signs.

What is the term used to describe the ability of machines to think independently?

Auto-Doc

This sounds like something from a TV show, but in the future the Auto-Doc machine could keep you in good health.

Sensors will analyze your breath and blood, or scan your body. After diagnosis, the Auto-Doc may be able to prescribe drugs or make pills.

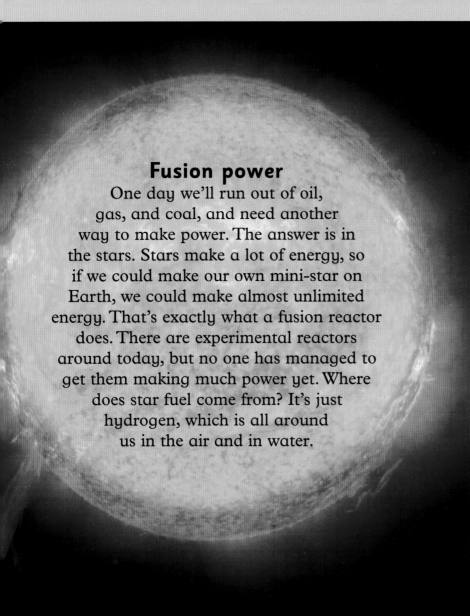

Fusion power

One day we'll run out of oil, gas, and coal, and need another way to make power. The answer is in the stars. Stars make a lot of energy, so if we could make our own mini-star on Earth, we could make almost unlimited energy. That's exactly what a fusion reactor does. There are experimental reactors around today, but no one has managed to get them making much power yet. Where does star fuel come from? It's just hydrogen, which is all around us in the air and in water.

Biome cars

Cars of the future will be environmentally friendly. Completely organic Biome cars will use special hybrid technology to release oxygen instead of carbon dioxide. This will reduce air pollution and greatly improve air quality. The car's body will be made of a material called BioFiber, specially grown in a laboratory.

True or false?

Can you figure out which of these facts are real and which are completely made up?

1 An LCD TV screen is made up of millions of tiny squares called pixels.

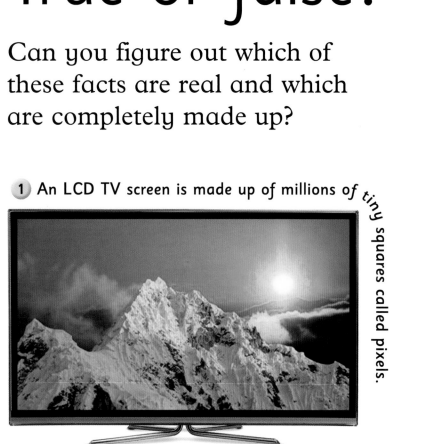

3 A cell phone converts sounds into radio waves.

2 In a lawnmower, three pistons go up and down to turn the wheels.

5: False—they are made of steel 6: True 7: False—it has a solid body

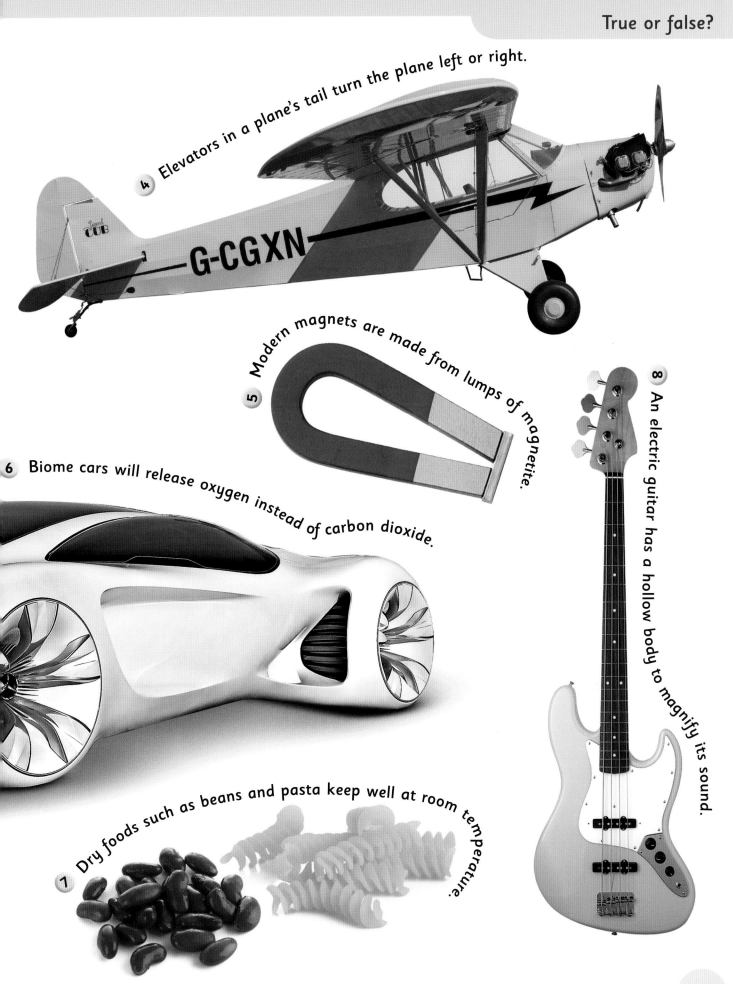

4 Elevators in a plane's tail turn the plane left or right.

5 Modern magnets are made from lumps of magnetite.

6 Biome cars will release oxygen instead of carbon dioxide.

7 Dry foods such as beans and pasta keep well at room temperature.

8 An electric guitar has a hollow body to magnify its sound.

Answers, 1: True 2: False—one piston goes up and down 3: True 4: False—the rudder does

Quiz

Test your knowledge
with these quiz questions.

4 What is the main arm of a crane called?

A. Trolley   B. Counterweight

C. Hydraulic ram   D. Jib

5 Steel structures that support cables carrying electricity are called...

A: Base stations   B: Towers

C: Turbines   D: Power stations

1 What did Sir Isaac Newton discover when an apple fell from a tree?

A. Radio waves   B. Gravity

C. Buoyancy   D. Thrust

6 What are the special robots used by search engines known as?

A. Worms   B. Scorpions

C. Spiders   D. Ladybugs

2 Brakes help vehicles do which of the following?

A. Stop moving   B. Change direction

C. Protect the driver D. Speed up

7 Where were smoke detectors first used?

A: Xanadu House   B: Oil drilling rigs

C: Lighthouses   D: *Skylab*

3 What captures energy from the sun to make electricity from it?

A: Iron rods   B: Solar panels

C: Magnets   D: Batteries

8 Up to how many passengers can an Airbus A380 carry?

A. 1,215   B. 853

C. 746   D. 543

9 What is the name of the fixed point around which a lever's solid part turns?

A. Pulley

B. Fulcrum

C. Load

D. Sprocket

10 Balloons float in the air when filled with which gas?

A: Helium

B: Oxygen

C: Carbon dioxide

D: Nitrogen

11 How many inventions did Thomas Edison patent?

A. 500

B. 253

C. 1,093

D. 670

12 What creates the orange flashes in fireworks?

A: Copper compounds

B: Lithium salts

C: Iron flakes

D: Calcium salts

13 Incandescent bulbs have filaments made of...

A: Steel

B: Lead

C: Tungsten

D: Silver

14 Which wireless system allows electronic gadgets to transmit data without plugging them into each other?

A. Bluetooth

B. FM Radio

C. GPS

D. Morse code

15 During a race, where does a Formula 1 car refuel and get new tires?

A. Garage

B. Track

C. Port

D. Pit stop

16 A picture that shows hot things as white and yellow, and cold things as blue, is called...

A: Photograph

B. Thermogram

C. Virtual screen

D. X-ray

Answers. 1:B 2:A 3:B 4:D 5:B 6:C 7:D 8:B 9:B 10:A 11:C 12:D 13:C 14:A 15:D 16:B

What am I?

Can you figure out what is being talked about from the clue?

Fire

2: I was invented in China more than 2,000 years ago.

High Wheeler

Cell phone

Wheel

Track-racing bike

1: I am a type of bicycle without gears and with pedals attached to my wheels.

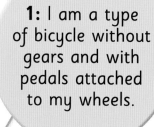

Diamond

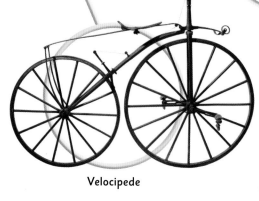

Velocipede

Biofuel

Mountain bike

126

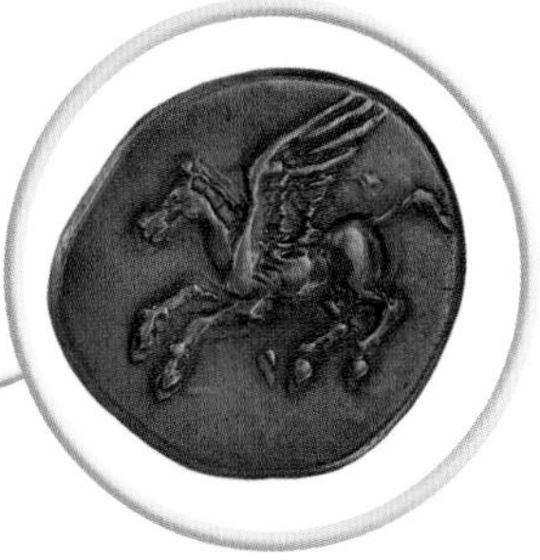

Coin

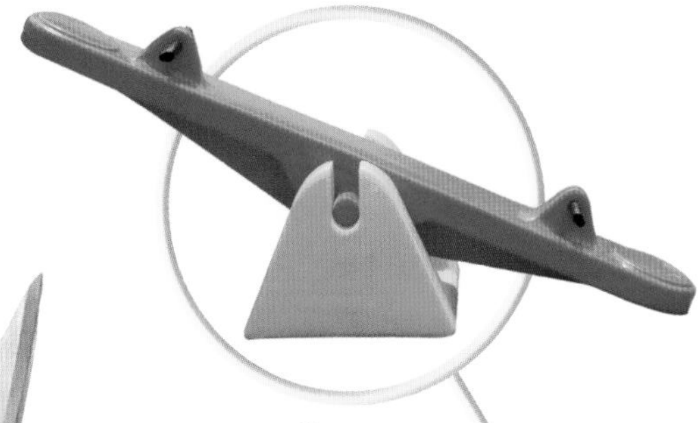

Seesaw

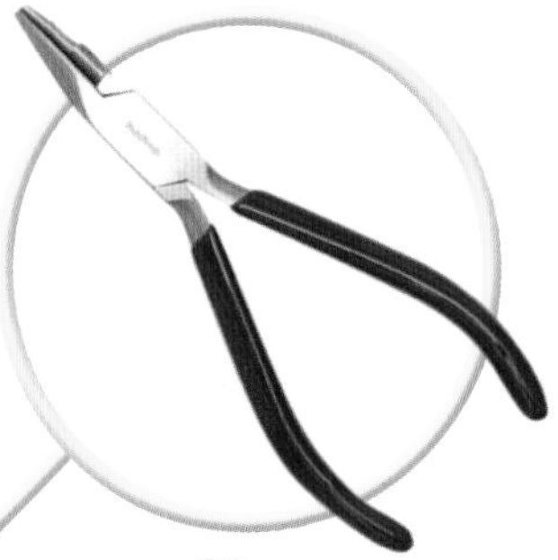

Pliers

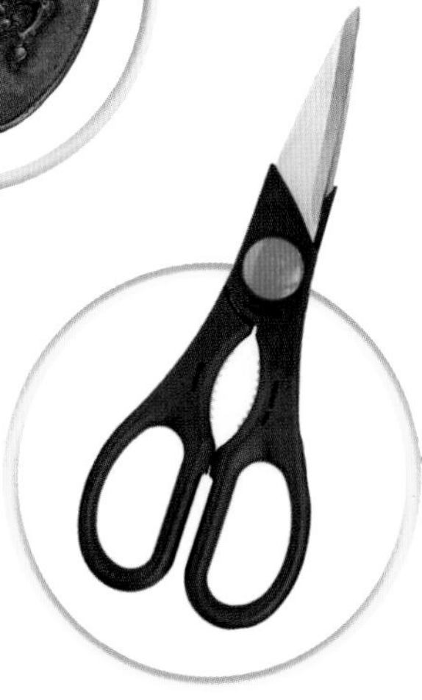

Scissors

3: Made of two class 3 levers, I reduce the force you apply.

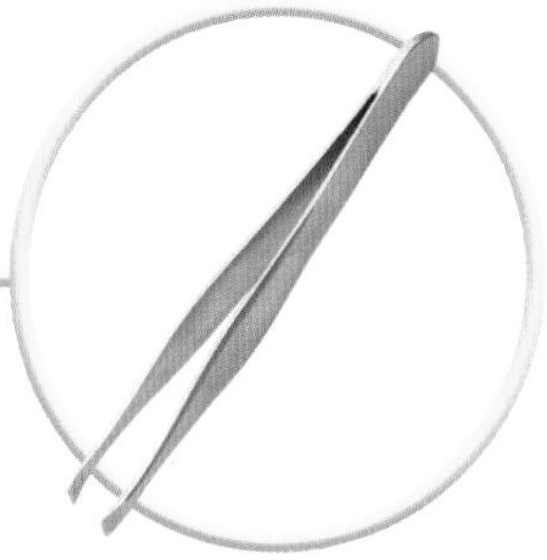

Tweezers

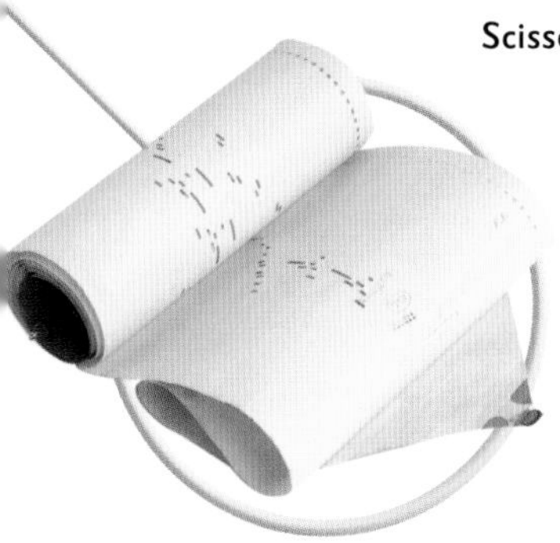

Paper

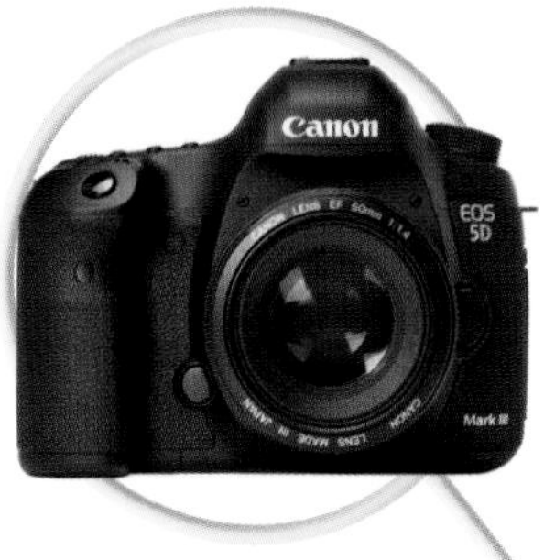

Camera

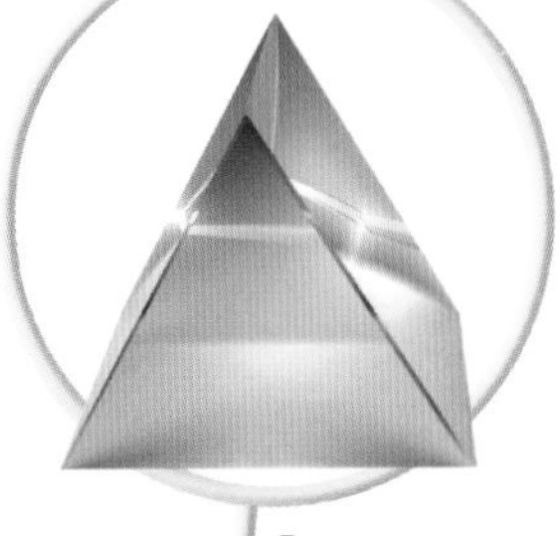

Prism

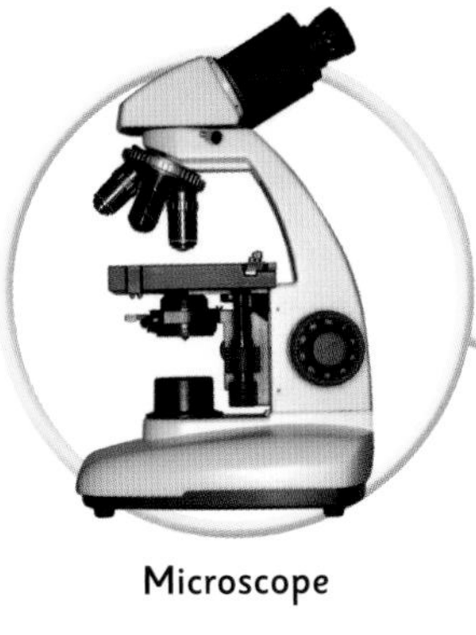

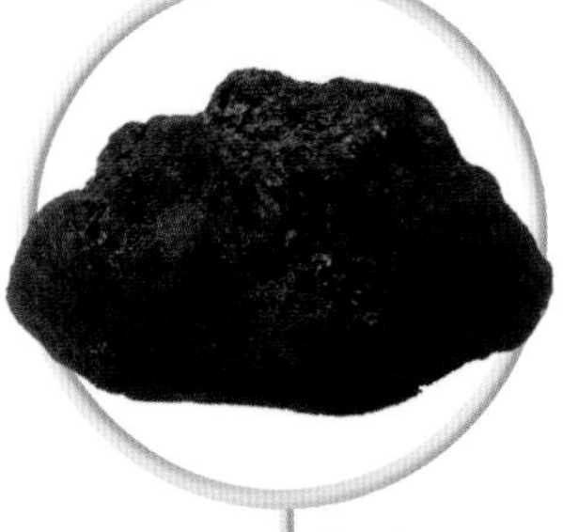

Microscope

Coal

5: I have a simple convex lens that makes things look bigger.

4: I am used as a fuel and can be found deep underground.

Wood

Magnifying glass

Answers: 1: Velocipede 2: Paper 3: Tweezers 4: Coal 5: Magnifying glass

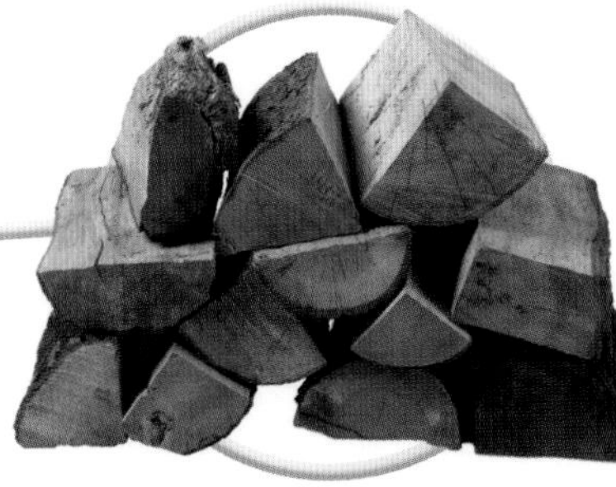

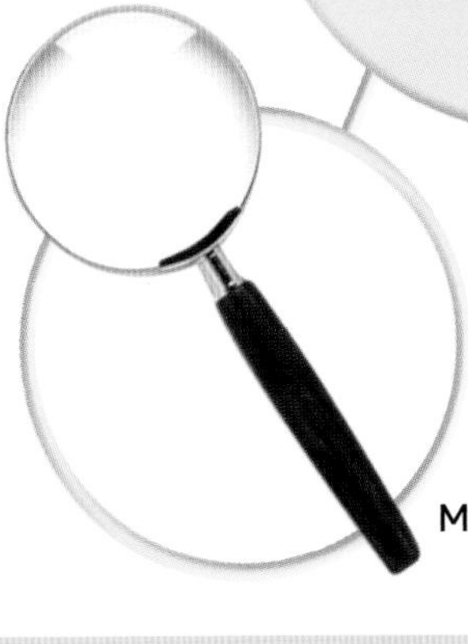

3: German mathematician Gottfried Leibniz developed the early version of this coding system.

1: Inspired by Morse code, US academic Bernard Silver invented this in 1948.

4: The design of this structure in England was based on the shape of an oak tree.

2: This structure in New York City is lit up by over 300,000 bulbs.

5: This instrument was invented in 1608 by Hans Lipperhay from Holland.

Where in the world?

Test your knowledge about where each of these was invented or found by matching the clues with the pictures.

Empire State Building

Bar code

Lodestone

Barossa Reservoir

Smeaton's Tower

Shoes

7: Lodestone 8: Shoes 9: Trans-Siberian Express 10: Bullet train 11: Compass 12: Barossa Reservoir

9: This train makes the world's longest journey of 5,857 miles (9,297 km).

6: In 1800, the Italian scientist Alessandro Volta invented this.

10: Operating in Japan, this is the world's first high-speed rail service.

8: People from Mesopotamia crafted these out of leather in 1500 BCE.

11: The Chinese invented this after discovering that a free-moving magnet will point north.

7: Discovered by Thales of Miletus, this naturally occurring object is thought to be made when lightning strikes.

12: If you whisper on one end of this structure in Australia, it can be heard clearly at the other end.

Battery

Bullet train

Compass

Binary code

Telescope

Trans-Siberian Express

Answers: 1: Bar code 2: Empire State Building 3: Binary code 4: Smeaton's Tower 5: Telescope 6: Battery

Glossary

accelerate To change velocity—the speed or direction. See *velocity*

aerodynamics Study of the way gases move (especially air), and the way things, such as airplanes, move in air

amplifier Something that makes a sound louder by increasing the power of an electrical signal

amplitude Height of a wave, such as a sound wave, from its peak (highest point) to its trough (lowest point). The bigger the amplitude, the more energy a wave has. A sound wave with a large amplitude is loud

atom Smallest particle of a particular element

biofuel Fuel made by or from living things. Wood, alcohol made from corn, and biogas made from garbage are all biofuels

binary code Code made up of the digits 1 and 0. Digital technology (computers) converts all letters and numbers into binary. For example, the letter "A" can be coded as 01000001

bit Smallest unit of memory used by a computer. The word "bit" is short for "binary digit"

buoyancy Upward force that acts on an object in liquid or a gas, affecting how well an object can float

byte Group of eight bits

carbon emissions Gases containing carbon that are released into the air, especially when fuel is burned. They may cause global warming

circuit Loop that an electric current travels around

concave When an object curves inward, like a bowl, it is concave

conductor Material that lets electricity or heat pass through. Metals are good conductors

convex When an object curves outward, like the back of a spoon, it is convex

coolant Liquid or gas that cools things down

current Flow of electricity from one place to another

data Another word for "information," especially digital information

decibel Unit that can be used to describe how loud sound is

density Mass of a solid, liquid, or gas in relation to its size. A dense material has lots of atoms packed closely together. Less dense objects float in more dense fluids. Wood can float in water because it is less dense than water

digital Describes a machine that works by using numbers. Digital watches display the time in numbers rather than on a dial. Digital technology, such as computers, stores data in binary code

displacement Amount of fluid (a liquid or gas) that is moved by an object placed in the fluid. An egg dropped into a glass of water will displace some water. The amount of water displaced has the same volume as the egg

What is g-force?

download To copy files from the Internet to your computer

drag Force that slows an object down as it moves through air or water. The faster the object moves, the more drag there is

efficiency How much of a machine's energy is turned into useful work. An energy-efficient lightbulb uses little energy to create a lot of light

electromagnet Magnet created by a flow of electricity through a coil

electron Tiny particle inside an atom. It carries a negative electric charge

element Chemical elements are substances that cannot be broken down into any other substances. Atoms in an element are all one kind—they all have the same number of protons

energy Ability to do things (such as walk or move an object). Something that can supply energy is called a power source

fiber-optic cable Flexible tube containing very thin, bendy glass fibers that carry information in the form of light waves

fluid Liquid or a gas. The atoms in a fluid can move freely to fill space

force Push or a pull. Gravity is the force that keeps you on the ground

fossil fuels Fuels that come from the earth and are the remains of living things. Coal, oil, and gas are all fossil fuels. They are not renewable sources of energy

friction Force that makes things slow down. When two solids rub against each other, or when a solid moves through liquid or gas, it causes friction

fulcrum Point, or pivot, that a lever turns on

gearwheel Wheel with "teeth" around the outside that can connect to and turn another gearwheel. A toothed wheel that connects to a chain is called a sprocket

geothermal power Power that comes from natural heat within the Earth

gravity Force that pulls objects toward one another. The pull of Earth on an object is called its weight

Fibre-optic cable

horsepower Unit used to measure a machine's power. It was first used to describe how powerful a steam engine was compared to a horse

hydraulic Hydraulic machines have pipes filled with liquids. Hydraulics help increase forces such as lifting, pulling, or pushing so a machine can work more efficiently

hydroelectric power Electricity that is made using the power of water, such as using a flowing stream to turn a turbine

The force of gravity on an object.

inertia Resistance of an object to a change in movement. An object that is stationary (not moving) will continue staying still, and an object that is already moving will keep moving in a straight line and not change direction, unless force is applied

insulator Material that does not let electricity or heat pass through it easily. Wood and plastic are insulators

internal combustion engine Engine that burns fuel inside itself to create power

kinetic energy Energy an object has when it moves. The faster it moves and the more mass it has, the greater its kinetic energy

LCD Stands for "liquid crystal display." LCD screens display pictures or numbers by applying an electric voltage to liquids that act like crystals

lens Object that bends light rays to make an image

lever Simple machine made up of a bar moving on a fulcrum. Using a lever magnifies or reduces a force to make a job easier. Seesaws, wheelbarrows, and tweezers are all levers

magnetic field Area around a magnet where other magnets are attracted or repelled

magnify To increase or make bigger

mass Amount of substance, or matter, that makes up an object

metadata Information (such as key words) in a computer file that describes the content. For example, a file of a picture might have metadata that tells you how big it is or when the picture was taken

microchip chip that contains transistors, which control the flow of electricity and then convert electric signals into computer language

molecule Two or more atoms joined together. A water molecule is made up of three atoms—two hydrogen atoms and one oxygen atom

momentum When an object is moving it has momentum. The more mass an object has and the faster it moves, the more momentum it has. The more momentum, the harder it is to stop the object from moving

motherboard Main circuit board of a computer or other large electronic gadget

nanotechnology Technology that can build things from atoms and molecules—the very smallest parts of an object or material

neutron Inside an atom's nucleus are neutrons and protons. Neutrons have no electrical charge

nuclear energy Power that comes from the energy released by the atoms of certain elements

nucleus Atoms are made up of a nucleus and electrons. The nucleus is made up of neutrons and protons

orbit Path an object in space takes around another. For example, the Earth orbits the sun

patent Official record of an invention that registers who made it so no one else can claim they did

photovoltaic panels Panels that collect solar energy (from sunlight) and turn it into electricity. They are also called solar panels

pixel Small, colored, square picture element that makes up part of a picture on a computer or television screen

potential energy Energy stored in an object that is raised above the ground. It changes into kinetic energy when the object falls

prism Triangular glass block used to split light into visible colors

What are turbines?

proton Inside an atom's nucleus are neutrons and protons. Protons have a positive electrical charge

pulley One or more wheels with a rope around it. It is used to move loads

reflection When light waves bounce off a surface (such as a mirror) and change direction, they are reflected

refraction When light waves travel through a transparent object (such as a window or glass prism), the light bends. This is refraction

renewable energy Power that comes from the sun, wind, water, or geothermal sources. Unlike fossil fuels, these will never run out

satellite Natural or mechanical object that moves around a planet. The moon is the Earth's natural satellite. Mechanical satellites circle the Earth and send back information on things like weather

solar power Power that comes directly from the sun

solution One substance dissolved in another

streamlined Objects with smooth curves. Air or water can flow over it with as little resistance as possible

technology Application of scientific methods, processes, and knowledge, often used to invent objects for everyday needs

thermostat Device that controls temperature, for example, on a radiator or a boiler

thrust Force that moves something forward. Engines provide thrust for planes and cars

transistor Part of an electric circuit that controls the flow of electricity

velocity Speed of a moving object in a particular direction

virtual reality Computer-generated environment that feels like real life to the person experiencing it

voltage Force that makes electrons move in an electric current.

wave Up-and-down or back-and-forth movement that carries energy from one place to another

weight Pull of gravity on an object gives the object weight. It is not the same as mass. An object's mass is the same wherever it is, but its weight can change, depending upon the force of gravity. An object weighs one-sixth as much on the moon as on the Earth

zero gravity Feeling like you are weightless, usually experienced in outer space

Machines with blades that turn when gas (such as air) or liquid flows past them.

Index

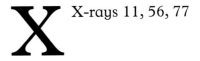

Picture credits

The publisher would like to thank the following for their kind permission to reproduce their photographs: (Key: a-above; b-below/bottom; c-center; f-far; l-left; r-right; t-top)

123RF.com: scanrail 11cr; sam74100 117tl; **Courtesy Mercedes-Benz Cars, Daimler AG:** 121br, 122-123c; **Courtesy of Motorcycle-USA.com:** 37br; **Alamy Images:** Aleksey Boldin 96bl, 96-97c; chombosan 118br, Design Pics Inc 100bl; Design Pics Inc 100bl; Russell Hart 100crb, imageBROKER 114, Alexey Kotelnikov 118cla, Robert Mora 104cl, 105cl, 127c, Science Photo Library 96c, 101tc, 101c, Tetiana Vitsenko / Iphone is a trademarks of Apple Inc., registered in the U.S. and other countries. 7br, 102cra, 122tr, 126ca; Ian Shaw 11crb, Mike Brand 128bc; 19th era 6cra; A Room with Views 7tl; Judith Aronson / Peter Arnold, Inc. 80tr; Roger Bamber 80-81ca; Stephen Bond 6tr; Mark Boulton 73cra (recycling point); Mike Brand 91bl; Scott Camazine 56bl; Chesh 92bl; Tony Cordoza 83cra (projector); David Noton Photography 15cr (crane), 18-19; Danita Delimont 8br; GabiGarcia 34b; Horizon International Images Limited 74-75 (sun and yellow sky); D. Hurst 7fbr, 49fbr, 123t; Leslie Garland Picture Library 19tr, 95crb (radio circuit), 106cra; Oleksiy Maksymenko 96ca, 103ca (phone battery); Mindset Photography 87cr; Motoring Picture Library 24tl; National Mot or Museum / Motoring Picture Library 61cra (central locking); David Pearson 21tr; Mark Phillips 73bl; PVstock.com 85tr; Rolf Hicker Photography 9br; Ian Shaw 11br; Adrian Sherratt 8cra (fire welding); Stockfolio 532 87br; Studioshots 105fclb; The Print Collector 26bl; Joe Tree 106br (digital radio); Colin Underhill 43cra (aircraft), 50-51 (main image), 126tc; Wolfgang Usbeck / Bon Appétit 68bc (chicken in oven), 68crb; View Stock 86clb; Tony Watson 37cb, 127b; WidStock 65tr; Jochem Wijnands / Picture Contact 58br; WildLife GmbH 79cr; Jerome Yeats 7cl; **Courtesy of Apple:** 96clb (trackpad), 96crb (hard drive); Photo: **Beiersdorf AG:** 13fbr (plaster); **Courtesy of Canon (UK) Ltd:** 95cr, 104tr (insert); **Corbis:** Westend61\Fotofeeling 124tr; A2070 Rolf Haid / DPA 52br, 53bl (insert); Mike Agliolo 98ca (background), 98cl, 99cr (background); Jeffrey Arguedas / EPA 23cra (truck), 29 (main image); David Arky 84cra (light bulb), 92tr; Bettmann 5tr, 6cl, 52clb, 107cla (photo inserts); Richard Broadwell / Beateworks 1cl, 64cr (light bulb); Burke / Triolo Productions 9cra; Car Culture 25clb, 39tr; Ron Chapple 63crb (corn), 67br; Chogo / Xinhua Press 41crb (Qinghai-Tibet railway); Claudius 43crb, 57crb (turbines -close up); Chris Collins 88br; Construction Photography 45br (brick), 63cra (hydroelectric power); Angela Coppola 120bl (boy); Jim Craigmyle 92c; Nigel J. Dennis / Gallo Images 89bl; Rick Doyle 32tr; Robert Essel NYC 81cra (rear-view mirror); Shannon Fagan 111b (boy with rabbit); Randy Faris / image100 64crb (recycling); Thomas Francisco 75cr, 81tl; Martin Gallagher 115fcra; Glowimages 87tr; Andrew Gompert / EPA 81br; Ole Graf 16-17cra (fulcrum), 16-17b (seasaw); Mike Grandmaison 63bl; Richard Gross 67tl; H et M / photocuisine 65br; Don Hammond 46-47 (main image); Philip Lee Harvey / Photoconcepts 120bl (grass); Dallas and John Heaton / Free Agents Limited 41cra (Bullet train); HO / Reuters 47tr; Hulton-Deutsch Collection 7cra (Sinclair C5), 7tc, 26cla, 26tl, 107tr; ImageShop 2cra; ION / amanaimages 93bl; The Irish Image Collection 65cla; Simon Jarratt 43br, 63cra (solar power), 67cra (solar power); Mark A. Johnson 63cr (tidal power); Karl-Josef Hildenbrand / DPA 113cra (search engine browser); Kulka / zefa 13cra (sheep); Patrick Lane / Somos Images 98l; Larry Lee Photography 65cra (insert); Larry Lee 48-49 (main image); Lester Lefkowitz 32ca; Leng / Leng 64cr (laundry); Ted Levine 32cla (diver); Barry Lewis 53cra, 65clb (flames); Yang Liu 57cr, 62tr; Gerd Ludwig 63cla; David Madison 25br; Sadao Maejima / AmanaImages 87tl; Lawrence Manning 6fbr, 27cra; MM Productions 64tr (gardening); Moodboard 12bl (light bulb), 23cb, 23cra (welder), 32cla (welder), 64cra (television); Noah K. Murray / Star Ledger 43cra, 52tr; Charles O'Rear 9bc (coins); David Papazian / Beateworks 64cra (insulation); Louie Psihoyos 95tc; Radius Images 62l; Nick Rains 41cra (Australian); Anthony Redpath 120fbl (rain); Jim Reed 89cl; Roger Ressmeyer 63crb (geothermal power), 67cb; Reuters 119bl; Michael Rosenfeld / DPA 2-3 (circuit board t & b); Schlegelmilch 35cl; Sie Productions 32fcla; Julian Smith 85cr; Paul A. Souders 57tl; Specialist Stock 47bc; Pauline St. Denis 64cra (walking); Hubert Stadler 25cra (waterwheel); George Steinmetz 1bl, 48crb (gas burning), 65bl; Keren Su 60crb; Ramin Talaie 119cla; Tetra Images 106fcla (microphone); Transtock 37cl; Bernd Vogel 103cla (man with phone); Karl Weatherly 75cra (rainbow), 77tl; Westend61 15cra (lake), 17tr; William Whitehurst 77cra; Bai Zhiyong / Xinhua Press 1br, 26-27c; **Dorling Kindersley:** Freddie Rogers 123t, The National Cycle Collection 122bc, The Science Museum, London 8tl, 129bc (compass), The University of Aberdeen 127tl, Toro Wheelhorse UK Ltd 122bl, Vikings of Middle England 128br; Anglo-Australian Observatory, photography by David Malin 60bl (galaxy background); British Library 10cla; Design Museum, London 89cra (vacuum cleaner); Exeter Maritime Museum, National Maritime Museum, London 8fclb; © Firepower, The Royal Artillery Museum, Woolwich 24cb; Glasgow Museum 11ca, 107ca (early television); London Planetarium 10ca; Marconi Instruments Ltd 75crb (oscilloscope screen), 89bc, 89ca; Mark Hall Cycle Museum, Harlow Council 26clb; Jamie Marshall 12fbl, 57bl, 105crb; Judith Miller / Wallis and Wallis 61ca (handbag); National Motor Museum, Beaulieu 11bl (early car), 31bl; National Railway Museum, York 40cla; Stephen Oliver 57cra (unlike poles), 60cra; David Peart 48crb (diver); Pitt Rivers Museum, University of Oxford 8cl; Anthony Pozner, Hendon Way Motors 81cr; Guy Ryecart, courtesy of Renault 57cl; Science Museum, London 4bc (Faraday's induction ring), 4bl (refractometer), 4bl (telephone), 4br (electric), 4br (spectacles), 4fbr (Wimhurst voltage), 5bl (teamaker), 5br (microscope), 5fbl (camera), 5fbr (radio amplifier), 6bc, 6bl, 8cb, 8cla, 8clb, 9fcra (compass), 10br, 11cla (Edison's lamp), 11fcla, 94cl, 95cl; Toro Wheelhorse UK Ltd 30bc; Paul Wilkinson 12cla (car), 23ca, 28bl; York Museums Trust (Yorkshire Museum) 9clb; **Electrolux:** 114tr; **Dreamstime.com:** Gawriloff 13cb, 97br, Mikhail Kokhanchikov / Mik122 134tc, Marekp 13ca, Yinan Zhang / Cyoginan 118clb; Alexander Pladdet 94bl, Alexandr Rutin 129br, Andrew Oxley 102bl, 103c, Anke Van Wyk 127tc, Bill Emrich 76bl, Clearviewstock 119t, Galyna Andrushko 122cl, Georgios Kollidas 99cl, Haiyin 117r, Ivan23g 103br, Ivansmuk 125bl, Kts 127cr, Manaemedia,\ iPad mini is a trademark of Apple Inc., registered in the U.S. and other countries. 11br, Manaemedia\iPhone is a trademark of Apple Inc., registered in the U.S. and other countries 102cr, Peter Wollinga 57fcrb, 65t, Raja Rc / Rcmathiraj 125cr, Sardorrr 122cl (Tv), Sergey Peterman 7bl, Sergiy Trofimov 129bc, Suchatsi 95bl, Trondur 64cl, Wayne0216 129bl, Wellphotos 114c, Yuriy Chaban 10cl; **Electronics and Computer Science, University of Southampton:** Rob Spanton (formica.ecs.soton.ac.uk) 115t ("Formica" bot); **Ernestomeda s.p.a.:** Zaha Hadid / DuPont™ Corian® / Scholtès - "Z. Island by DuPont™ Corian®" 116cra; **Getty Images:** Noah Berger / AFP 118crb, Krisztian Bocsi / Bloomberg 103br, Alexey Bubryak 27crb, Robert Daly 101cb, David Madison 37br, Andrey Rudakov / Bloomberg 38tr, Westend61 27br; Bloomberg 115br, Werner Forman 8bl; AFP 31br; Colin Anderson / Photographer's Choice 22l; artpartner-images / Photographer's Choice 96-97 (background); Rob Atkins / Photographer's Choice 15crb (crane close-up), 19tc; Benelux Press 95br, 114b (main image); Don Bishop / Photodisc 113cra (computer); Alex Cao / Photodisc 6-7; Frank Chmura / Nordic Photos 43crb (power lines), 59br; Tony Cordoza 107bl (TV); Crowther & Carter / Stone 110-111 (background); Davies and Starr / Stone 113crb (tags); Peter Dazeley / Photographer's Choice 83cla (ice cream); Mary Kate Denny / Photographer's Choice 87crb (green); Digital Vision / George Diebold 67bl; Digital Vision / John William Banagan 87crb (red); 11crb; Michael Dunning / Photographer's Choice 77fbl; Laurence Dutton 103cra; Ben Edwards 81cra (dental mirror); Joshua Ets-Hokin / Photodisc 17tl; Don Farrall / Photodisc 6cla; Joe Fox / Photographer's Choice 76br; Gerard Fritz / Photographer's Choice 112-113 (background); Adam Gault / OJO Images 83cra (microscope); Dave Greenwood / Photonica 16cra (tweezers); Karl Grupe / Photonica 117cra; Darrell Gulin 105cla (camera screen), 105tc (pixel insert); Alexander Hafemann / iStock Exclusive 63cra (wind power); Bruce Hands 40cra; Tim Hawley / Photographer's Choice 113bl; Chris Hondros 4cra (camera film.); Lyn Hughes 43 (background), 45l (sky background); Hulton Archive 4tr, 10cb; Janicek 73cra (battery); Brian Kennedy / Flickr 40bl; Keystone / Stringer / Hulton Archive 52c; Romilly Lockyer / The Image Bank 42 (clouds background); Vincenzo Lombardo / Photographer's Choice 16cra (door handle); Steve McAlister 22cra, 113crb (document); Ian Mckinnell 4cra (pool ball); Ian Mckinnell / Photographer's Choice 13crb; Ryan McVay / Photodisc 25cra (steering wheel); Ryan McVay / Photodisc 6br; Ryan McVay / Stone 88bl; Jose Maria Mellado 20c; Steve Mercer / Photographer's Choice 113cra ('http'); Peter Miller 70-71 (snow flakes); Jo Mind / Stone 104bl; MJ Rivise Patent Collection 4cl; Brur Muff / Photographer's Choice 97tr; NASA / Science Photo Library 79tc; Hans Neleman 34tr; Joseph Niepce / Hulton Archive 10cra; noa images / Digital Vision 113cr; Thomas Northcut / Digital Vision 75clb; Thomas Northcut / Stockbyte 84fclb; Jose Luis Pelaez 77bl; PhotoLink / Photodisc 61crb (lightning in insert); Pier / Stone 87crb (yellow); Pier / Stone 75crb (sparks); PM Images 13cr (wheelchair); Steven Puetzer / Photodisc 84clb; Terje Rakk 41crb (brakes); RNHRD NHS Trust 13cr (x-ray); Lauri Rotko 15cl; Chad Slattery / Stone 53tc; Stocktrek Images 36tl, 119cb; Paul Taylor 15br, 20cra; The Image Bank / Garry Gay 87crb (orange); Travelpix Ltd / Photographer's Choice 84-85b; **HES Energy Systems:** 118cra; **iStockphoto.com:** 13tr, 36cb (cyclist), 61cra (credit card), 81 (face in mirror), 102tl (modern mobile phone), 106cl (digital radio transmitter), 106l (digital radio transmitter & background), 107cr (transmission icons), 112ca; Kseniya Abramova 36-37b (horses); Arndt Design 41bl; Black Ink Designers 106br (sound waves); Sascha Burkard 76bc; Caziopeia 103clb (3/4 angle mobile); Kenneth Cheung 102ftl; CreativeChain Design House 104-105t (background); Elton Dralle 28cr; Blaz Erzetic 1clb, 109tc; Jamie Farrant 90cb (speaker insert); Nadezda Firsova 10C 101 (background); Robert Hadfield 81crb (sunglasses); Jaap Hart 84-85t (ray background); Er Ten Hong 22crb (petrol, diesel and electricity icons); Stiv Kahlina 55cb; Kathy Konkle 107cra (camera); Mosquito 103bl; Shane O'Brien 106fclb (radio); Tomasz Pietryszek 37tr; T. Popovc 104br, 105clb; Vladimir Popovic 58ftl; Laurent Renault 36bl; Petr Stepanov 117cla; Mark Swallow 7bl; Jeremy Voisey 73cra (chemical hazard warning triangle); stockdev / Getty Images Plus 55c, JulNichols 73crb, Mark Kostich 77br, PhonlamaiPhoto 42clb, StockRocket 100cr; **Peter Zelei 9tr; Kingspan Off-Site:** 72r; **NASA:** 43cr, 60bl, 119br, 119tr; Finley Holiday Films 48br; Bill Ingalls 54c, 54crb; SOHO / EIT Consortium / ESA 121tl; **Photolibrary:** 40clb; Hufton + Crow 72bl; Javier Larrea 41tl; Bruno Morandi / Robert Harding Travel 41cr (Trans-Siberian Express); Doug Plummer 102cl; **Press Association Images:** Peter Morrison 115clb; **Reuters: Science & Society Picture Library:** Science Museum 11tl, 13br (socks); **Science Photo:** 24br, 44bl, 83cr (contracted pupil); AJ Photo / Hop Americain 90bl; Andrew Lambert Photography 94crb; Alex Bartel 116-117b (house BSIP, Chassenet 83crb (dilated pupil); Dr. Jeremy Burgess 78crb; Pascal Goetgheluck 91crb, 105br (eye); Gustoimag 57br, 70-71 (fridge x-ray), 95crafdav, 103c; Roger Harris 99tl; Mehau Kulyk 88tl (wave background), 92-93t (background), 103tc; Lawrence Lawry 79b, 122-123b; Andy Levin 56br; R. Maisonneuve, Publiphoto Diffusion 91tc; Jerry Mason 103cla (disassembled mobile phones); Will & Deni McIntyre 85clb; Medical Rf.com 83ca (eye ball), 120tr; Peter Menzel 38br (insert); New York Public Library / Humanities & Social Sciences Library 106tl (Marconi); David Parker 74tl; Philippe Psaila 78l; Pasqual Sorrentino 9tl; Andrew Syred 80bl; Takeshi Takahara 44tr; David Taylor 75cra (light interference), 79tl; Sheila Terry 24bc; Detlev van Ravenswaay 11tc, 55br; **SuperStock:** Prisma 41cra (TGV); © **2009 Universal Orlando Resort All Rights Reserved:** 53br; **University of Washington:** Babak Parviz 117tr; **Worldwide Aeros Corp.:** 121b; **UNSW Solar Racing Team, Sunswift:** 38b.

All other images © Dorling Kindersley
For further information see: www.dkimages.com

Acknowledgments
Dorling Kindersley would also like to thank: Francis Bate, Greg Foot, Leon Gray, Jennifer Lane, Chris Oxlade, Jon Woodcock, and Katie Lawrence for editorial assistance, and Seeta Parmar for proofreading. And thanks to Robert Spanton and Klaus-Peter Zauner from ECS, University of Southampton, for information on Formica robots.